THE WIT & WISDOM OF
MOVIES

To the future of British cinema. May it one day rise from the ashes and bite Hollywood's complacent, fat backside.

First Edition (as *The Wit & Wisdom of the Movies*)
© 2005 House of Raven

This edition published in 2011 by Prion
An imprint of
Carlton Books Limited
20 Mortimer
London W1T 3JW

Typeset in Minion Pro and Frutiger 55
First edition design: David Coventon

ISBN: 978-1-85375-846-1

Printed in China

THE WIT & WISDOM OF THE
MOVIES

**More than 800 amusing, enlightening
and downright disheartening quotations**

PRION

"The cinema has no boundaries."

So said Orson Welles, one of cinema's finest artists. This breadth of scope makes compiling a book of movie quotes a difficult task; cinema presents us with life and all its foibles and idiosyncrasies, and has further license to explore possibilities beyond what we already know and accept as real. This fantasy element is crucial; cinema for most viewers is an escape from the mundane and the humdrum.

Some directors choose to reflect the gritty urbanity of everyday life, but, significantly, far more of them show us a view beyond our own horizons. This escape doesn't need to be a bold, futuristic or historical landscape, like Blade Runner or Spartacus; it can just as readily be the brief connection between two characters en passant, like Sullivan's Travels or Lost In Translation.

We hope to have provided a collection of quotes which appeals to all sorts of moviegoer. Many of the quotes are from familiar films, and will raise a smile or a nod of recognition. There are plenty that will be less familiar, that are thought-provoking and witty and may create a desire to explore a film the reader may have missed. There is more than a passing nod to the classics, and the great names of Hollywood's heyday; but we are not stuck, Halliwell-like, in a rose tinted world where nothing can ever be as good as it used to be. We have tried to avoid snobbery, too; the primary function of cinema is to entertain. Skillful trash makes for infinitely better viewing than earnest ennui.

Deciding how to section the book was hard. A-Z by speaker is unsatisfactory, and allows for no continuity; the same applies to presenting the quotes by film. A chronological running order would have made some sense – it is interesting to see how both dialogue and attitudes have changed so dramatically as movies developed. In the end we opted for themes, to allow that continuity, and to allow us to create some neat juxtaposition of contrary or similar viewpoints.

At heart there are only four themes in all major art forms, cinema included; family, love, power, death. These themes are too broad; most great movies take in three if not all four of these "big ideas."

A brief word of warning: there is no artificial "bleeping" of the industrial language in some of the quotes. Swearing, whatever one's views on the subject, is rife in modern cinema, and has been for over thirty years. To produce a publication which pretends it doesn't happen would be nonsense, and would ignore the fact that good writers use profanity for effect and emphasis with great skill. Shakespeare, for example.

N.B. • Each quote that appears in the book is numbered (i.e. •1234).
These numbers run sequentially throughout the book.
Use the index at the back to find films by title.
• Both American and English spellings have been used throughout the book as appropriate.

I would like if I may,
to take you on a
strange journey…

Charles Gray narrating **The Rocky Horror Picture Show** [1]

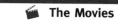

Talking films are a very interesting invention, but I do not believe that they will remain long in fashion. *Louis-Jean Lumiere* •2

I have determined that there is no market for talking pictures. *Thomas Edison* •3

It will never be possible to synchronize the voice with the picture. *D.W.Griffith, 1926* •4

They are spoiling the oldest art in the world; the art of pantomime. They are ruining the great beauty of silence.
Charlie Chaplin on the advent of talkies •5

One of the first things I noticed was that whenever I smiled or let the audience suspect how much I was enjoying myself, they didn't seem to laugh as much as usual. *Buster Keaton* •6

Why should people go out and pay money to see bad films, when they can stay home and see bad television for nothing?

Samuel Goldwyn •7

Pictures are entertainment, messages should be delivered by Western Union.

Samuel Goldwyn •8

I can't see what Jack Warner can do with an Oscar; it can't say yes.

Al Jolson •9

…an eruption of trash that has lamed the American mind and retarded Americans from becoming a cultured people…

Ben Hecht on cinema •10

Life, every now and then, behaves as though it had seen too many bad movies, when everything fits too well – the beginning, the middle, the end – from fade-in to fade-out.
Bogart as Harry in **The Barefoot Contessa** •11

Joe Gillis: You're Norma Desmond!
You used to be in silent pictures. Used to be big.
Norma: I am big. It's the pictures that got small.
William Holden and Gloria Swanson in **Sunset Boulevard** •12

At least the old moguls had the courage of their convictions and the authority to act on them. Today they're terrified of making decisions. You have to have eight meetings even to order the toilet paper.
Bryan Forbes •13

The cinema has no boundaries. It's a ribbon of dream. *Orson Welles* •14

Film was, and is still, a romantic business, just as life is romantic.
Katharine Hepburn •15

The main thing is, if you talk too much, the audience won't remember anything. So say something short and memorable. *Steve McQueen* •16

One of the joys of going to the movies was that it was trashy, and we should never lose that.
Oliver Stone •17

People sometimes say that the way things happen in the movies is unreal, but actually it's the way things happen in real life that's unreal. *Andy Warhol* •18

Nobody should come to the movies unless he believes in heroes.
John Wayne •19

The film is the best of all media, you can do marvels with it.
Henry Miller •20

Life in the movie business is like the beginning of a new love affair: it's full of surprises and you are constantly getting fucked. *David Mamet* •21

If a person can tell me the idea in twenty-five words or less, it's going to make a pretty good movie.

Steven Spielberg •22

In movies, it doesn't really matter if you're good. It matters if the audience likes you.

John Malkovich •23

Some of the worst films of all time have been made by people who think too much.

Steven Soderbergh •24

You know what the problem with Hollywood is? They make shit. Unbelievable, unremarkable shit. Now I'm not some grungy wannabe filmmaker that's searching for existentialism through a haze of bong smoke or something. No, it's easy to pick apart bad acting, short-sighted directing, and a purely moronic stringing together of words that many of the studios term as "prose". No, I'm talking about the lack of realism. Realism; not a pervasive element in today's modern American cinematic vision.

John Travolta as Gabriel in **Swordfish** •25

16

Patti: Couldn't we just once see a nice, quiet movie
where boy meets girl, they have problems which aren't
too weird, they fall in love, and live happily ever after?
Canoe: Now, why would you want to see a lot of
unhealthy stuff like that?
Hayley Mills and Tom Lowell in **That Darn Cat!** •26

Popcorn is the last area of movie business where good taste is still a concern. *Vincent Canby* •27

I see my films as first aid to the modern male psyche. Masculinity
is becoming obsolete. Most jobs today can be held by women.
Many men have become defensive and enjoy being taken
to another time, another period, when masculinity was
important to survival. *Clint Eastwood* •28

I finally figured out today's movie rating system: G means
the hero gets the girl; R means the villain gets the girl;
and X means everybody gets the girl. *Kirk Douglas* •29

Now, the pictures are too realistic. The brutality and
the nudity and the swearing — it's all too harsh.
Henry Hathaway •30

17

Violence in the movies is like drugs. The more of it you have, the more you want.
Wim Wenders •31

The concept of Merchant Ivory movies is foreign to America: there's no sex, nothing gratuitous or violent.
Gwyneth Paltrow •32

If it's in focus, it's pornography.
If it's out of focus, it's art.
Linda Hunt as Billy Hunt in **The Year of Living Dangerously** •33

In the first you use just the feather, in the second you use the whole chicken.
Roman Polanski on the difference between eroticism and pornography •34

I'll tell you a secret. The last act makes the film. Wow them in the end, and you've got a hit. You can have flaws, problems, but wow them in the end, and you've got a hit.
Brian Cox as Robert McKee in **Adaptation** •35

Strip away the phoney tinsel off Hollywood
and you'll find the real tinsel underneath.
Oscar Levant •36

I'm not very keen on Hollywood.
I'd rather have a nice cup of cocoa, really.
Noel Coward writes home •37

If you want to make it in this town,
you have to talk loudly and chew gum.
Anthony Hopkins on how to succeed in Hollywood,
according to actress Kelly Macdonald •38

I've been in Hollywood over 50 years.
I have watched Tinseltown vacillate
between despair and fear.
Billy Wilder •39

Paradise with a lobotomy.

Neil Simon on Hollywood •40

19

A trip through a sewer in a glass bottomed boat.

Wilson Mizner on Hollywood •41

Hollywood, land of contrasts: where any day you can see the very rich rubbing shoulders with the rich. *Kenneth Tynan* •42

They don't want films in Hollywood. What they want is a soundtrack they can sell.
Peter Mullan •43

A dreary industrial town controlled by hoodlums of enormous wealth. *S.J.Perelman on Hollywood (attrib)* •44

If you stay away from parties, you're called a snob. If you go, you're an exhibitionist. If you don't talk, you're dumb. If you do talk, you're quarrelsome. Pardon me while I change my nail polish.
Lana Turner on Hollywood social life •45

I think that people need something to look up to, and Hollywood was the only Royalty that America ever had.
Bette Davis •46

The biggest electric train set any boy ever had!

Orson Welles, on the RKO studios •47

The only "ism" Hollywood believes in is plagiarism.
Dorothy Parker•48

The thing about Hollywood is, you have to be grateful to be working with thieves and liars, because the alternative is idiots. *David Ambrose* •49

Hollywood must be the only place on earth where you can get fired by someone wearing a Hawaiian shirt and a baseball cap. *Steve Martin* •50

The execs don't care what color you are, they care how much money you make. Hollywood is not really black or white; it's green. *Will Smith* •51

Hollywood is full of rather sleazy, unscrupulous people. Los Angeles is where they make deals and do business in the classic corporate American way – which is screw everybody and do whatever you can to make the biggest profit.

George Lucas •52

Being in Hollywood is like being in the Christian right these days. It's very, very right wing, no matter how much they claim they're Democrats and they're fighting for Barack Obama. I was in Hollywood a lot in the build-up to the Iraq war and there wasn't anybody who was against it. It was as if the American people were unable to access anything outside that bubble of cinematic reality. *Rupert Everett* •53

Giving your book to Hollywood
is like pimping your daughter.

Tom Clancy •54

Seeing your book turned into
a movie is like watching your
children get raped by Cossacks.

Kathy Lette •55

It's an opportunity to fly first class,
be treated like a celebrity, sit around
the pool and be betrayed.

Ian McEwan on working in Hollywood •56

23

Nobody's done anything to my book. It's right up there on the shelf. Hollywood mangles movies, not books.

James M. Cain, when asked if Hollywood had mangled his book, **The Postman Always Rings Twice** •57

I can't think of any film that improved on a good novel, but I can think of many good films that came from very bad novels.

Gabriel Garcia Marquez •58

Howard Hawks: Make him sound more like a pharaoh.
William Faulkner: I don't know how a pharaoh talks.

Discussing the script to **Land of the Pharaohs** •59

If it's well done, it's ignored. If it's badly done, people call attention to it.

William Goldman on screenwriting •60

There is no such thing as a good script, only a good film, and I'm conscious that my scripts often read better than they play.

Alan Bennett •61

I think nobody writes down. Garbage though they turn out, Hollywood writers aren't writing down. That is their best. *Dorothy Parker* •62

Whatever your script is like… if the punters don't want to sleep with the star, you may never be asked to write another one.

Richard Curtis •63

Michelangelo, make up your mind, once and for all: do you want to finish that ceiling?

Scriptwriting from hell from **The Agony & The Ecstasy** •64

What did I think of Titanic? I'd rather have been on it.

Miles Kruger •65

Several tons of dynamite are set off in this picture; none of it under the right people.

critic James Agee on **The Tycoon,** *1947* •66

Table for Five would be an ideal movie to watch on a plane; at least they provide free sick bags.

Simon Rose •67

27

Then came *Easy Rider,*
a disaster in the history
of film… *David Thomson, critic* •68

Camille with bullshit. *Alexander Walker on* **Love Story** •69

Love Story:
Die, witch! Die!

Joe Queenan, failing to reach for the Kleenex •70

They only got two things right
in *Lawrence of Arabia:* the camels
and the sand. *Lowell Thomas* •71

Forrest Gump is roughly as truthful about the world of intellectual handicap as *The Little Mermaid* is about fish. *Christopher Tookey* •72

Lonesome Cowboy is Andy Warhol's best movie to date, which is like saying a three-year-old has graduated from smearing faeces on the wall to the occasional use of finger paints.
*A review in **Variety** magazine* •73

On and on it goes, 140 minutes of tranquilising non-drama. Is there anything to wonder at in its journey to the centre of an ego? Only this — that Julia Roberts, one of the more thoughtful film stars, should have chosen to play the tremulous nincompoop herself. *Anthony Quinn in **The Independent** on **Eat, Pray, Love** (2010)* •74

DeMille made small-minded pictures on a big scale.
Pauline Kael •75

Movies are so rarely great art that if we cannot appreciate the great trash we have very little reason to be interested in them. *Pauline Kael* •76

The words "Kiss Kiss Bang Bang" which I saw on an Italian movie poster, are perhaps the briefest statement imaginable of the basic appeal of movies. *Pauline Kael* •77

Find a formula and milk it until it moos with pain.
Dorothy Parker •78

The unique thing about Margaret Rutherford is that she can act with her chin alone. Among its many moods I especially cherish the chin commanding, the chin in doubt, the chin at bay.
Kenneth Tynan •79

The critics? No, I have nothing but compassion for them. How can I hate the crippled, the mentally deficient, and the dead?
Albert Finney as Sir in **The Dresser** •80

For a critic, that first step is his first critic joke. People laugh.
Whole new world opens up. He makes another joke, and another,
and then one day, along comes a joke that shouldn't be made
because the show he is reviewing is a good show, but the joke
happens to be a good joke, and, you know what? The joke wins.
Richard Haydn as Alfred North in **Please Don't Eat The Daisies**•81

In America it is considered a lot more important
to be a great Batman than a great Hamlet.
Kevin Kline •82

Actually, I am a golfer. That is my real occupation.
I never was an actor; ask anybody, particularly the critics.
Victor Mature •83

I, along with the critics,
have never taken myself
very seriously. *Elizabeth Taylor* •84

Fuck the critics. They're like eunuchs. They can tell you how to do it, but they can't do it themselves. *Harry Cohn* •85

This pretentious, ponderous collection of religious rock psalms is enough to prompt the question, "What day did the Lord create *Spinal Tap,* and couldn't he have rested on that day, too?" *Rob Reiner as Marti DiBergi reads a review of the band's latest album* •86

Anything except that damned mouse.

King George V expresses his cinematic preferences. •87

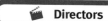

Every film should have a beginning, a middle and an end, but not necessarily in that order.
Jean-Luc Godard •88

Cinema should make you forget you're sitting in a theatre.
Roman Polanski •89

All you need for a movie are a gun and a girl.

Jean-Luc Godard •90

All I need to make a comedy is a park, a policeman and a pretty girl.

Charlie Chaplin •91

The Holy Ghost was working through me on this film, and I was just directing traffic.

Mel Gibson on his role in **The Passion of Christ** •92

Moviemaking is pointing the camera at beautiful women.
François Truffaut •93

A film director's total work
is a diary kept over a lifetime.
François Truffaut •94

A film is a petrified fountain of thought.
Jean Cocteau •95

Pick up a camera. Shoot something. No matter how small, no matter how cheesy, no matter whether your friends and your sister star in it. Put your name on it as director. Now you're a director. Everything after that you're just negotiating your budget and your fee. **James Cameron** •96

Moviemaking is the process of turning money into light. All they have at the end of the day is images flickering on a wall.
John Boorman •97

No art passes our conscience in the way film does, and goes directly to our feelings, deep down into the dark rooms of our souls. *Ingmar Bergman* •98

I couldn't comprehend the enormity of the experience, I wasn't really able to digest it in one sitting. I actually walked out of the theatre stunned and speechless. I didn't quiet understand the impact the film had on me until months later. It pulverised me. It was a miracle, that picture. *Steven Spielberg on David Lean's* **Lawrence of Arabia** •99

To me style is just the outside of content, content the insides of style, like the inside and outside of the human body – they can't be separated. *Jean-Luc Godard* •100

What is the moral of Icarus? "Don't fly too close to the sun?" Or is it, as I choose to believe, "Build better wings." *Stanley Kubrick* •101

You can put Eisenstein up with Michelangelo and Da Vinci. *Peter Greenaway* •102

I think it's very harmful for movie-makers to
see movies, because you either imitate them
or worry about not imitating them.
Orson Welles •103

Any director who doesn't believe in miracles isn't a realist.
Billy Wilder •104

No man ever said to his wife,
"Let's go and see this picture, the
director brought it in under budget."
Billy Wilder •105

If you see a man come through a doorway,
it means nothing. If you see him coming
through a window, that is at once interesting.
Billy Wilder •106

To me, there's no failure. This is all an exploration.

Indie film-maker John Sayles •107

There are no rules in film-making.
Only sins; and the cardinal sin is dullness.
   Frank Capra •108

To make a film is to improve on life, arrange it to suit oneself.
François Truffaut •109

I like the old masters, by which I mean
John Ford, John Ford and John Ford.
Orson Welles on his favourite directors •110

If there's specific resistance to women making movies, I just choose to ignore that as an obstacle for two reasons: I can't change my gender, and I refuse to stop making movies. *Kathryn Bigelow •111*

He's unstoppable. For every film he makes, there are a thousand more that play in his head. His cranium houses the world's largest multiplex cinema and it is open all hours, every day.

Tom Hanks on Stephen Spielberg •112

I filmed the truth as it was then. Nothing more.
Leni Riefenstahl, criticised as a Nazi collaborator •113

You don't rehearse — everything's a take.
Ricky Tomlinson on Ken Loach •114

Motivation? Say the fucking words.
Your motivation is your salary.

Roman Polanski to Faye Dunaway on the set of **Chinatown** •115

To Raoul Walsh a tender love scene is burning down a whorehouse.

Jack L Warner •116

We never do any research. Ethan
says research is for sissies.

Joel Coen •117

You know you're successful when they
make porno versions of your films.
They remade *Edward Scissorhands*
as *Edward Penishands*.

Tim Burton •118

I pride myself on the fact that my work has no socially redeeming value.

John Waters •119

I have never met anyone as utterly mean as Marilyn Monroe. Nor as utterly fabulous on the screen, and that includes Garbo.

Billy Wilder •120

While photographing the screen test which led to Marilyn Monroe's first studio contract, I got a cold chill. This girl had something I hadn't seen since silent pictures. She had a kind of fantastic beauty like Gloria Swanson, and she radiated sex like Jean Harlow. She didn't need a soundtrack to tell her story.   *Leon Shamroy* •121

However confused or difficult she is in real life, for the camera she can do no wrong.

Allan Snyder on Monroe •122

A sex symbol becomes a thing. I just hate to be a thing. But if I'm going to be a symbol of something, I'd rather have it sex than some other things they've got symbols of.   *Marilyn Monroe* •123

I said to Marilyn Monroe, "Why can't you get here on time, for fuck's sake?" And she replied, "You have that word in England, too?"

Laurence Olivier •124

I think it was the only ending for Marilyn, and I think she knew it.

George Cukor •125

Being a sex symbol is a heavy load to carry, especially when one is tired, hurt and bewildered.

Clara Bow •126

I am known in parts of the world by people who've never heard of Jesus Christ.

A characteristically modest Charlie Chaplin •127

In those days the public wanted us to live like Kings and Queens. So we did. Why not? We were in love with life.

Gloria Swanson •128

He can do nothing which is not worth watching.

Graham Greene on James Cagney •129

She has sex, but no particular gender. Her masculinity appeals to women, and her sexuality to men.

Kenneth Tynan on Dietrich •130

The fellow is the world's greatest actor. He can do with no effort what the rest of us spent years trying to learn; to be perfectly natural. *John Barrymore on Gary Cooper* •131

With him acting was an act of childbirth. What he needed was not so much a director as a midwife.

Alexander Korda on Charles Laughton •132

I might offend morals, but never good taste, the more important of the two.
Tallulah Bankhead •133

Can't act, can't sing, slightly bald. Can dance a little.

Fred Astaire's first screen test comment (apocryphal) •134

Bette Davis was my heroine. She used cigarettes so dramatically. *Lauren Bacall pays tribute* •135

He gives her class and she gives him sex.

Katharine Hepburn on Fred and Ginger •136

The great thing about Errol was that you always knew precisely where you stood with him because he always let you down.

David Niven on Errol Flynn •137

I always knew that if all else failed I
can become an actor. And all else failed.

David Niven •138

Working with Jimmy Stewart in *It's A Wonderful Life* was
very demanding. He's so natural, so realistic, that I never
knew whether he was talking to me or doing the scene.
Donna Reed •139

Being a star has made it possible for me to get
insulted in places where the average negro
could never hope to get insulted.

Sammy Davis jnr •140

I give hope to the hopeless. People look at me and say:
"If he can make it, I can be Queen of England."

Robert Mitchum •141

There are three things I never saw Elizabeth Taylor do — tell a lie, be unkind to anyone and be on time.

Mike Nichols on Liz Taylor •142

If someone was stupid enough to offer me a million dollars to make a picture — I was certainly not dumb enough to turn it down.

Elizabeth Taylor •143

I know darned well that if it weren't for those kids I wouldn't be able to own a car. I'm one guy in Hollywood who realises those kids pay my salary.

Alan Ladd appreciates his fans •144

Actors are fools to complain about the public's attention. They should be glad to have it, not claim they dislike it, and yet go out of their way to seek it.

So does Gregory Peck •145

My epitaph would be: "Here lies Gandalf. He came out." *Sir Ian McKellen* •146

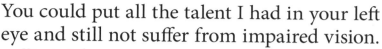

You could put all the talent I had in your left eye and still not suffer from impaired vision.
Veronica Lake •147

It's like meeting God without dying.
Dorothy Parker on Orson Welles •148

I really don't know who I am. Quite possibly, I do not exist at all.
Alec Guinness •149

With its unaccustomed rhythm and singsong cadence that develops into a flat drawl ending in a childlike query, it has the quality of heartbreak.
Cecil Beaton on the voice of Audrey Hepburn •150

Everyone wants to be Cary Grant. Even I want to be Cary Grant.
Cary Grant •151

I don't mind that I'm fat. You still get the same money.
Marlon Brando •152

The important thing in acting is to able to laugh and cry. When I have to cry, I think of my love life. When I have to laugh, I think of my love life.
Glenda Jackson, related by Kim Basinger •153

Julie Andrews has that wonderful British strength that makes you wonder why they lost India. *Moss Hart* •154

He had the menacing presence of an unexploded bomb.
Philip French on George C Scott •155

I told Robert De Niro he was a class-A bastard. He said, "I don't mind being a bastard, as long as I'm an interesting bastard." *Liza Minnelli* •156

I'm going to be a great film star! That is, if booze and sex don't get me first.
Liza Minnelli as Sally Bowles in **Cabaret** •157

Live? I can't go on live! I'm a movie star, not an actor.
Peter O'Toole in **My Favourite Year** •158

All Burt Reynolds has to do is wink at the camera and he's a star. I'm short and ugly and really have to act.
Dustin Hoffman •159

Dear boy, you look absolutely awful. Why don't you try acting? It's so much easier.

Laurence Olivier (attrib). This was Olivier's response to Dustin Hoffman depriving himself of sleep for 3 nights to replicate the exhaustion felt by his character in **Marathon Man** •160

Frank Ellroy: Why do you always wear the sunglasses?
Jack Nicholson: Without them, I'm fat and fifty. With them, I'm Jack Nicholson. *Jack Nicholson's secret to looking cool* •161

I don't go for this method acting stuff. I'm never going to be Meryl Streep. But then, she'll never be a Dolly Parton neither.
Dolly Parton •162

I gave my best performance, perhaps, during the war —
pretending to be an officer and a gentleman. *Alec Guinness in self-deprecating mode* •163

Daniel Day-Lewis has what every actor in Hollywood wants; talent. And what every actor in England wants; looks.
Gielgud pays homage •164

Accents? I can do Irish, Welsh, Manchester, Liverpool, Birmingham, Cockney and New York Jewish lesbian.
Julie Walters •165

Acting is not the things you say, it's the things you don't say.
Judi Dench •166

If you're pretty and you're working class you have an easier time. *Helena Bonham-Carter* •167

As a lifelong member of the non-pretty working classes, I would like to say to Helena Bonham-Carter: shut up, you stupid cunt. *Kathy Burke, in Time Out* •168

I live a privileged life. I'm rich. I'm happy. I have a great job. It would be absurd to pretend that it's anything different. I'm like a pig in shit.
Julia Roberts •169

If you ask any of my leading ladies they would tell you that they loved me. They should, because they have all given their best performances of their lives opposite me.
Michael Douglas epitomises Hollywood narcissism. •170

Talking about preparation is all hogwash; it takes the mystery out of the movies. I don't want to know how some guy wore the same socks for months to prepare for a role; then when I see the movie that's all I can think about – dirty socks.
Sean Penn •171

Fortunately, I was raised in such a way that I know that family and friends and dogs and flowers and walks are what's important about life, not movies and fame.
Gwyneth Paltrow. Ain't that sweet. •172

Sidney's more than a bass player. He's a fabulous disaster; he's a symbol, a metaphor. He embodies the dementia of a nihilistic generation. He's a fuckin' star.

David Hayman as Malcolm McLaren in **Sid and Nancy** •173

It's just I… I'm so tired of being admired all the time. All these men I mean… they're all beautiful, artistic minds, great sex, the whole package, but hollow, you know what I mean? I feel nobody's really honest with me. Nobody wants me for me.
Lara Flynn Boyle as Helen Jordan in **Happiness** •174

I'd rather watch old Doris Day movies than the Oscars. *Orson Welles* •175

I am very, very gobsmacked.
Emma Thompson, Best Actress •176

I am full of joy like a watermelon. I will explode. I cannot restrain this joy.
Roberto Benigni accepting a BAFTA •177

Cor! This is living, ain't it?
Brenda Blethyn, receiving an award at Cannes •178

It's just a meat parade in front of an international television audience.

George C Scott on the Oscar ceremonies – he declined his award for **Patton** •179

I'm not knocking the Academy Awards, I'm just saying that there's no actual cultural value to them – they're no judge of quality.
James Mason •180

The Oscars seems to have been confused with the Nobel Peace Prize.
Janet Maslin, on **Gandhi** *winning eight Oscars* •181

I thought I might win for *The Apartment* but then Elizabeth Taylor had her tracheotomy.
Shirley MacLaine •182

I can't stand the sight of Ronald Reagan — I'd like to stick my Oscar up his ass.
Gloria Grahame on the one-time US President •183

53

I'd like to finish with a word of warning. You may have started something. The British are coming.

*Colin Welland, Best Screenplay, **Chariots of Fire**. They weren't.* •184

I didn't even know there were such awards. I have people around me whose job it is not to tell me about such things.

*John Travolta, on winning the Golden Raspberry for Worst Actor of the Year (for **Battlefield Earth**, not his best!)*•185

Reporter: Is there any award left for you to win? Judi Dench: There's still Crufts. *Judi Dench, having gone barking mad* •186

54

The only thing that separates us from the animals is our ability to accessorise. *Olympia Dukakis in* **Steel Magnolias** •187

I don't want to be a traitor to my generation and all but I don't get how guys dress today. I mean, come on, it looks like they just fell out of bed and put on some baggy pants and take their greasy hair – ugh – and cover it up with a backwards cap and we're supposed to swoon? I don't think so.

Alicia Silverstone as Cher in **Clueless** •188

You could toss a bolt of fabric at Carol Lombard, and however it would land on her she would look smart. *Travis Banton* •189

I notice you don't have any tattoos. I think that's a wise choice. I don't think Jackie Onassis would have gone as far if she'd had an anchor on her arm.

Steve Martin as Fire-Chief C.D. Bales in **Roxanne** •190

I see split ends are universal. Lost in space with no conditioner, eh?

Julie Brown as Candy in **Earth Girls Are Easy** •191

This is 1852 dumplin', 1852, not the Dark Ages. Girls don't have to simper around in white just because they're not married.

Bette Davis as Julie in **Jezebel** •192

I've got a major wedgie.

Sarah Michelle Gellar as Daphne in **Scooby Doo** •193

Just because I wear a uniform doesn't mean I'm a girl scout.

Shirley MacLaine as Fran Kubelik in **The Apartment** •194

Michael: Do you get to wear a tutu?
Billy: Fuck off, they're only for lasses.
I wear me shorts.
Michael: You ought to ask for a tutu.
Billy: I'd look a right dickhead.
Michael: I think you'd look wicked.

Stuart Wells and Jamie Bell in **Billy Elliott** •195

Rob, I'm telling you this for your own good, that's the worst fuckin' sweater I've ever seen, that's a Cosby sweater.

Jack Black as Barry in **High Fidelity** •196

That dress does things for you.
Doesn't do me any harm, either.

Bob Hope as Peanuts to Hedy Lamarr in **My Favorite Spy** •197

That's quite a dress you almost have on.

Gene Kelly in **An American In Paris** •198

Celeste (seeking approval on her dress):
Is this acceptable?
Steven: Is the drool apparent?

Kim Basinger and Dan Aykroyd in **My Stepmother Is An Alien** •199

How did you get into that dress?
With a spray gun? *Bob Hope as Hot Lips Burton to*
Dorothy Lamour in **Road To Rio** •200

Big Boy Caprice: Around me, if a woman
doesn't wear mink, she don't wear nothing.
Breathless Mahoney: Well, I look good both ways.

Al Pacino and Madonna in **Dick Tracy** •201

58

Verna: I'd look good in a new coat, honey.
Arthur: You'd look good in a shower curtain.
Virginia Mayo and James Cagney in **White Heat** •202

You'd look good in a paper napkin.
Frank Sinatra as Tony Rome to Raquel Welch in **Lady In Cement** •203

When it gets hot like this, you know what I do? I keep my undies in the icebox! *Marilyn Monroe as The Girl in* **The Seven Year Itch** •204

No mistake, I shall regret the absence of your keen mind. Unfortunately it is inseparable from an extremely disturbing body.
Gary Cooper to Barbara Stanwyck in **Ball of Fire** •205

With a binding like you've got, people are going to want to know what's in the book.
Gene Kelly to Leslie Caron in **An American In Paris** •206

I suppose it wasn't meant to be. I mean, he does dress
better than I do. What could I bring to the relationship?
Alicia Silverstone as Cher in **Clueless** •207

Wayne: She's a babe.
Garth: She's magically babelicious.
Wayne: She tested very high on the stroke-ability scale.
Mike Myers and Dana Carvey wax lyrical about Claudia Schiffer in **Wayne's World** •208

Have I got nice tits,
or have I got nice tits?
Emily Lloyd as Lynda in
Wish You Were Here •209

She should get the Oscar for
best bust. Anyone with those
two floaters doesn't need
a lifeboat. *Camille Paglia on Kate Winslet's*
assets in **Titanic** •210

Harris: Sandee, your breasts feel weird.
Sandee: That's because they're real.
Steve Martin and Sarah Jessica Parker in **L.A.Story** •211

My breasts are full of love and life. My hips are round and well apart.
Such women, they say, have sons. *Elizabeth Taylor as Cleopatra* •212

I look like a Russ Meyer movie.
Kirstie Alley as Mollie in **Look Who's Talking** •213

Hal: Does she take the cake, or what?
Mauricio: She takes the whole bakery, Hal.
Jack Black introduces the enormous version of Gwyneth Paltrow to Jason Alexander in **Shallow Hal** •214

Anti-wrinkle cream there may be, but anti-fat-bastard cream there is not. *Mark Addy in The* **Full Monty** •215

When you are called a character actor, it is because you're too ugly to be called a leading lady. *Kathy Burke* •216

It's not a pretty face, I grant you, but underneath its flabby exterior is an enormous lack of character.
Oscar Levant as Adam Cook in **an American in Paris** •217

She has a face that belongs to the sea and the wind, with large rocking-horse nostrils and teeth that you just know bite an apple every day. *Cecil Beaton on Katharine Hepburn* •218

When I was growing up, I knew I was different. The other girls were blonde and delicate, and I was a swarthy six-year-old with sideburns.
Nia Vardalos as Toula in **My Big Fat Greek Wedding** •219

When nine hundred years old you will reach, look as good you will not, mm?

Frank Oz as Yoda in **Return of the Jedi** •220

I don't think I have the kind of face that makes an audience love you.

Meryl Streep •221

I have a face that would stop a sundial.

Charles Laughton •222

That man's ears make him look like a taxi cab with both doors open.

Howard Hughes on Clark Gable •223

Men who wear glasses are so much more gentle and sweet and helpless. Haven't you ever noticed it? They get those weak eyes from reading, you know, those long, tiny little columns in the Wall Street Journal. *Marilyn Monroe in* **Some Like It Hot** •224

Lady, you certainly don't look like
somebody that's just been shipwrecked.

Tallulah Bankhead fails to convince in **Lifeboat** •225

…haunting, handsome, almost beautiful, yet…
irreducibly funny. *James Agee on Buster Keaton's face* •226

The most striking of her features is her whiteness, which would put
the moon or a white rabbit to shame. Instead of eyebrows she has
limned butterflies' antennae on her forehead.

Cecil Beaton on Marlene Dietrich •227

Being a sex symbol has to do with attitude, not looks. Most
men think it's looks, most women know otherwise.

Kathleen Turner •228

What kind of dish was she?
The 60c special? Cheap, flashy;
strictly poison under the gravy?

Charles McGraw as Walter Brown in **The Narrow Margin** •229

Men pay homage to my beauty
and show no interest in me. *Hedy Lamarr* •230

I'm not offended by dumb blonde jokes because
I know I'm not dumb, and I know I'm not blonde.
Dolly Parton •231

You look about as much like a boy as Mae West.
Joel McCrea as Sullivan, not impressed with Veronica Lake's disguise in **Sullivan's Travels** •232

All my life I wanted to look like Liz Taylor. Now
I find that Liz Taylor is beginning to look like me.
Drag queen, Divine •233

I'm afraid there's less to me than meets the eye.
Michael Caine as Frank Bryant in **Educating Rita** •234

It sort of cools the ankles, doesn't it?
Marilyn Monroe in **The Seven Year Itch,** *adopting that
classic pose over a subway grate.* •235

Each time I wear black, or like, lose my temper, or
say anything about anything, you know, they always
go, "Oh it's so French. It's so cute." Ugh! I hate that!
Julie Delpy as Celine in **Before Sunrise** •236

Why didn't you take off all your clothes?
You could have stopped forty cars.
Clark Gable to Claudette Colbert in **It Happened One Night** •237

I want to look good naked!
Kevin Spacey as lester Burnham in **American Beauty**
explains why he wants to go to the gym •238

Nudity on the stage? I think it is disgusting,
shameful and damaging to all things American.
But if I were 22 with a great body, it would be
artistic, tasteful, patriotic and a progressive,
religious experience. *Shelley Winters* •239

Katharine Hepburn runs the gamut of emotions from A to B.

Dorothy Parker •240

Doris Day is as wholesome as a bowl of cornflakes and at least as sexy.

Dwight Macdonald, US critic •241

To know her is not necessarily to love her.

Rex Reed on Barbra Streisand •242

Take away the pop eyes, the cigarette and those funny clipped words and what have you got?

Joan Crawford on her old chum, Bette Davis •243

What annoys me most? Unused fireplaces, pink sweet peas, badly made beds… and Miriam Hopkins. *Bette Davis* •244

Greta Garbo is hermaphroditic, with the cold quality of a mermaid.

Tennessee Williams •245

Her face could launch a thousand dredgers.

Jack De Manio on Glenda Jackson •246

Meryl Streep can act Polish or English or Australian but she sure as hell can't act blonde.

Joan Bennett •247

Los Angeles is full of pale imitations of Pamela Anderson and, worse still, Pamela Anderson herself.

Lisa Marchant •248

He's the only person I know
who's in worse shape than I am.

Marilyn Monroe on Montgomery Clift during filming of **The Misfits** •249

…he looks like an assistant master
at some inferior private school. Glasses
and bad teeth. *Harold Nicholson on Leslie Howard* •250

The rudest man I ever met, and unattractive
— pock-marked as an Easter Island statue.

Broadcaster Libby Purves on Richard Burton •251

One of the biggest shits I've ever come
across in show-business. He was just a pig.

Jeffrey Bernard on Yul Brynner •252

Bob Hope will go to the opening of a phone
booth in a gas station in Anaheim, provided
they have a camera and three people there.

Marlon Brando •253

Darling, they've absolutely ruined your perfectly dreadful play!

Tallulah Bankhead to Tennessee Williams •254

We were both in love with George Sanders.

Zsa Zsa gabor on her former husband •255

Kirk Douglas would be the first man to tell you he's a difficult man. I would be the second.

Burt Lancaster •256

What do you mean, heart attack? You've got to have a heart before you can have an attack.

Billy Wilder, about Peter Sellers •257

Jean-Claude van Damme exudes the charisma of a packet of Cup-a-Soup.
Jonathan Romney •258

A second rate bicycle acrobat who should have kept his mouth shut.
Kingsley Amis on Charlie Chaplin •259

Arnold Schwarzenegger's body is like a condom full of walnuts.
Clive James •260

At least I can wear high heels again.
Nicole Kidman after her divorce from Tom Cruise •261

He's not an actor, he's a special effect.

Jonathan Coe on Arnold Schwarzenegger •262

Reporter: Has the success of *Titanic* changed your husband?
Linda Hamilton: No, he's always been a jerk.

Newshound and the former Mrs James Cameron •263

Katharine Hepburn: Thank goodness
I don't have to act with you any more.
John Barrymore: I didn't know you ever
had, darling. *The loving couple, after filming*
A Bill of Divorcement •264

Mia Farrow? I always knew Frank would end up in bed with a boy.

Ava Gardner is disparaging about ex-husband, Frank Sinatra's, latest squeeze •265

You're so vain /
You probably think
this song is about you.

Carly Simon's song, reputedly about Warren Beatty •266

Warren Beatty has an interesting psychology. He has always fallen in love with girls who have just won or been nominated for an Academy award.

Leslie Caron •267

It's a damn good thing he never co-starred with Lassie. *Shirley MacLaine on Warren Beatty's wandering eye* •268

Mr Carter, if the headline is big enough, it makes the news big enough.
Orson Welles as Charles Foster Kane in **Citizen Kane** •269

Where I work, we have only one editorial rule. We can't write anything longer than the average person can read during the average crap. *Jeff Goldblum as Michael in* **The Big Chill** •270

Make them cry. Make them laugh. Make them mad, even mad at you. Stir them up and they'll love it, and come back for more, but, for heaven's sake, don't try to improve their minds. *John Ireland as Jack Burden in* **All the King's Men** •271

Television is not the truth. Television is a goddamn amusement park. *Peter Finch as Howard Beale in* **Network** •272

The world will see only what I show them.
Anthony Hopkins as **Nixon** •273

In a conspiracy like this, you build from the outer edges, and you go step by step. If you shoot too high and miss, everybody feels more secure. *Hal Holbrook as the undercover contact, Deep Throat, in* **All the President's Men** •274

The likelihood of one individual being right increases in direct proportion to the intensity with which others are trying to prove him wrong. *James Mason as Jordan in* **Heaven Can Wait** •275

Hauk: Sir, the man has got an irreverent tendency. He did a very off-color parody of former VP Nixon.
General Taylor: I thought it was hilarious.
Hauk: Respectfully, sir, the former VP is a good man and a decent man.
Gen Taylor: Bullshit! I know Nixon personally. He lugs a trainload of shit behind him that could fertilize the Sinai. Why, I wouldn't buy an apple from the son of a bitch and I consider him a good, close, personal friend.
Bruno Kirby and Noble Willingham in **Good Morning, Vietnam** •276

Greed… is good! Greed is right! Greed works! Greed clarifies, cuts through, and captures the essence of the evolutionary spirit… Greed… will save the USA. *Michael Douglas as Gordon Gekko in* **Wall Street** •277

I don't feel we did wrong in taking this great country away from the Indians. Our so-called stealing of this country from them was just a matter of survival. There were great numbers of people who needed new land, and the Indians were selfishly trying to keep it for themselves. *The ever sensitive John Wayne* •278

John Wayne… was late to show his political potential. If I had known then what I know now, I think I would have shot him dead on the spot. *Jean Arthur* •279

John Wayne actually got angry at me when I abandoned my tough-guy image to play the tormented artist Vincent van Gogh off in Lust for Life… it was like I was not being true to my people. I said, "Duke, we're actors. We just create the illusion of these big macho guys. You know, John, you really didn't win all those wars." But we obviously didn't see eye to eye. He actually thought he was John Wayne. *Kirk Douglas* •280

Frost: Are you really saying the President can do something illegal?
Nixon: I'm saying that when the President does it, it's not illegal.
An exchange between interviewer David Frost (Michael Sheen) and former US President Richard Nixon (Frank Langella) from Frost/Nixon •281

From what I can see, no matter what system of government
we have, there'll always be leaders and always be followers.
Gary Cooper as Longfellow Deeds in **Mr Deeds Goes To Town** •282

Acting is not the noblest profession in the world. There are
things lower than acting – not many, mind you. The politicians
give you something to look down on from time to time.
Spencer Tracy •283

Power is when we have every justification to kill and we don't.
That's what the Emperor said. A man stole something. He's
brought in before the Emperor; he throws himself down on
the ground. He begs for mercy. He knows he's going to die.
And the Emperor pardons him. *Liam Neeson as Oskar Schindler
in* **Schindler's List** •284

Well you look about the kind of angel I'd get. Sort of a fallen
angel, aren't you? What happened to your wings?
James Stewart as George Bailey in **It's A Wonderful Life** •285

In Italy they had 30 years under the Borgias: terror, murder, blood-
shed. They produced Michelangelo, Leonardo da Vinci,
and the Renaissance. In Switzerland they had brotherly love,
500 years of democracy and peace, and what did they produce
— the cuckoo clock! *Orson Welles as Harry Lime in* **The Third Man** •286

Within your 'purview'? Where do you think you are, some fucking regency costume drama? This is a government department, not a fucking Jane fucking Austen novel. Allow me to pop a jaunty little bonnet on your purview and ram it up your shitter with a lubricated horse cock! *Malcom Tucker (Peter Capaldi) displays his matchless grasp of political debate in* **In The Loop** •287

King Arthur: The Lady of the Lake, her arm clad in the purest shimmering samite held aloft Excalibur from the bosom of the water, signifying by divine providence that I, Arthur, was to carry Excalibur. That is why I am your king. Dennis the Peasant: Listen, strange women lyin' in ponds distributin' swords is no basis for a system of government. Supreme executive power derives from a mandate from the masses, not from some farcical aquatic ceremony. *Graham Chapman and Michael Palin in* **Monty Python and the Holy Grail** •288

I love that word "relationship". Covers all manner of sins, doesn't it? I fear that this has become a bad relationship. A relationship based on the President taking exactly what he wants and casually ignoring all those things that really matter to Britain. We may be a small country but we're a great one, too. The country of Shakespeare, Churchill, the Beatles, Sean Connery, Harry Potter. David Beckham's right foot. David Beckham's left foot, come to that. And a friend who bullies us is no longer a friend. And since bullies only respond to strength, from now onward, I will be prepared to be much stronger. And the President should be prepared for that. *Hugh Grant as the British Prime Minister in* **Love, Actually.** •289

Peace of mind! I have no peace of mind. I have had no peace of mind since we lost America. Forests, old as the world itself, plains, strange delicate flowers, immense solitudes. And all nature new to art. All ours. Mine. Gone. A paradise lost.

Nigel Hawthorne as King George III in **The Madness of King George** •290

Observe, Lord Burghley, I am married… to England.

Cate Blanchett as **Elizabeth** •291

Why, Richard, it profits a man nothing to give his soul for the whole world – but for Wales? *Paul Scofield as Thomas More in*
A Man For All Seasons •292

Antonius Block: Wait a moment.
Death: That's what they all ask.
I grant no reprieves.

Max Von Sydow and Bengt Ekerot in **The Seventh Seal** •293

79

I can't say I'm flatly against killing under any circumstances.
I would kill in defence of my own family. I could kill in
self-defense, I suppose. And I could kill if somebody invaded
my country. But to kill Vietnamese, to slaughter them wholesale,
in an undeclared War against other Vietnamese halfway around
the world, at the request of a corrupt puppet regime that doesn't
reflect the will of its own people – that I couldn't do. That kind
of war I consider not only illegal but immoral.
Paul Newman. Rien ça change, Paul. •294

I don't want to go into politics.
I want to do some good in the world.
Alan Alda •295

Kill everyone now! Condone first degree murder!
Advocate cannibalism! Eat shit! Filth is my politics!
Filth is my life! *Divine as Babs Johnson in* **Pink Flamingos** •296

You know what? You're an individual, and that makes
people nervous. And it's gonna keep making people
nervous for the rest of your life. *Rosie O'Donnell as Ole Golly in*
Harriet The Spy •297

80

Woman in bar: Hey, Johnny, what are you rebelling against?
Johnny: What've you got?
Marlon Brando keeps his options open in **The Wild One** •298

I am involved. We are all involved. Mom, a boy was killed tonight. I don't see how I can get out of that by pretending it didn't happen. *James Dean as Jim Stark in* **Rebel Without A Cause** •299

Sailor: My snakeskin jacket... Did I ever tell you that this here jacket represents a symbol of my individuality and my belief in personal freedom?
Lula: About fifty thousand times.
Nicolas Cage and Laura Dern in **Wild At Heart** •300

There is no right or wrong. There is only fun and boring.

Fisher Stevens as The Plague in **Hackers** •301

This whole world's wild at heart and weird on top.
Laura Dern as Lula in **Wild At Heart** •302

I'll never be mellow, OK? I'd rather be dead than mellow.
You might as well take me out and shoot me in the back
of the head before I'm gonna be mellow.

Mickey Rourke talking like a true hell-raiser •303

K-Mart sucks!

Dustin Hoffman as Raymond Babbitt in **Rain Man** •304

Finch: Why do you wanna work on television?
Bridget: I've got to leave my job because I shagged my boss.
Finch: Fair enough. Start on Monday.

Neil Pearson and Rene Zellweger reacha prompt agreement in **Bridget Jones' Diary** •305

This rabble you're talking about, they do most of the working
and paying and living and dying in this community. Well is
it too much to have them work and pay and live and die in
a couple of decent rooms and a bath? Anyway my father
didn't think so, people were human beings to him. But to
you, a warped, frustrated old man, they're cattle. Well in
my book he died a much richer man than you'll ever be.

James Stewart as George Bailey in **It's A Wonderful Life** •306

82

Everything begins and ends at exactly the right time and place.

Anne Lambert as Miranda in **Picnic At Hanging Rock** •307

How come we only ask ourselves the really big questions when something bad happens?

Mark Wahlberg as Tommy Corn in **I Heart Huckabees** •308

Blame is for God and small children.

Dustin Hoffman as Dega in **Papillon** •309

Faith is believing in things when common sense tells you not to.

Maureen O'Hara as Doris Walker in **Miracle on 34th Street** •310

God always has another custard pie up his sleeve.

Lynn Redgrave as Georgy in **Georgy Girl** •311

As long as the prerequisite for that shining paradise is ignorance, bigotry and hate, I say the hell with it.

Spencer Tracy as Henry Drummond, on Heaven, in **Inherit The Wind** •312

They may torture my body, break my bones, even kill me. Then they will have my dead body, not my obedience.

Ben Kingsley as **Gandhi** •313

An eye for an eye only ends up making the whole world blind.

Ben Kingsley as **Gandhi** •314

Dad always used to say the only causes worth fighting for were the lost causes.

James Stewart as Jefferson Smith in **Mr Smith Goes To Washington** •315

They work so hard at living, they forget how to live.

Gary Cooper, as Longfellow Deeds in **Mr Deeds Goes To Town,**
comments on the denizens of New York •316

Tomorrow, you'll know I wasn't kidding and you'll think I was crazy, but look, I figure it this way: better to be king for a night than schmuck for a lifetime.

Robert De Niro in **King of Comedy** •317

We think too much and feel too little. More than machinery we need humanity. More than cleverness we need kindness and gentleness.

Charlie Chaplin in **The Great Dictator** •318

Sometimes you just have to toot your own horn, otherwise nobody'll know you're comin'.

Dolly Parton as Dr Shirlee Kenyon in **Straight Talk** •319

Real loss is only possible when you love something more than you love yourself.

Robin Williams as Sean in **Good Will Hunting** •320

If you think being an ordinary person is any easier than being an extraordinary one, you're wrong.
Rachel Griffiths as Hilary Du Pre in **Hilary and Jackie** •321

Hearts will never be practical until they can be made unbreakable.
Frank Morgan as **The Wizard of Oz** •322

Well, whatever you do, however terrible, however hurtful, it all makes sense, doesn't it, in your head? You never meet anybody that thinks they're a bad person. *Matt Damon as Tom Ripley in* **The Talented Mr Ripley** •323

I love how wine continues to evolve, how if I open a bottle the wine will taste different than if I had uncorked it on any other day, or at any other moment. A bottle of wine is like life itself — it grows up, evolves and gains complexity. Then it tastes so fucking good. *Virginia Madsen as Maya in* **Sideways** •324

If I could only have one food for the rest of my life? That's easy. Pez. Cherry flavor Pez. There's no doubt about it.
Jerry O'Connell as Vern in **Stand By Me** •325

Dunking's an art. Don't let it soak so long. A dip and plop, into your mouth… It's all a matter of timing. I ought to write a book about it. *Clark Gable as Peter Warne in* **It Happened One Night** •326

It's not the despair. I can cope with the despair. It's the hope I can't stand.
John Cleese as Headmaster Brian Stimpson in **Clockwise** •327

There is a difference between knowing the path and walking the path.
Laurence Fishburne as Morpheus in **The Matrix** •328

Money won is twice as sweet as money earned.

Paul Newman as Eddie Felson in **The Color of Money** •329

Do you know what "nemesis" means? A righteous infliction of retribution manifested by an appropriate agent. Personified in this case by an 'orrible cunt... me. *Alan Ford as Brick Top in* **Snatch** •330

Sometimes I'm not sure there's ever been an America. I just think it's all been Frank Capra films. *John Cassavetes* •331

The saddest words in the world are "it might have been."

Alec Guinness as Henry Holland
in **The Lavender Hill Mob** •332

To be overly honest in a dishonest world is like
plucking a chicken against the wind... you'll
only wind up with a mouth full of feathers.
Lou Jacobi as Moustache in **Irma La Douce** •333

If you just learn a single trick, Scout, you'll get along a lot better
with all kinds of folks. You never really understand a person until
you consider things from his point of view... Until you climb
inside of his skin and walk around in it. *Gregory Peck as Atticus Finch*
in **To Kill A Mockingbird** •334

Never stray from the path, never eat a windfall apple and
never trust a man whose eyebrows meet in the middle.
Angela Lansbury as Granny gives good advice in **The Company of Wolves** •335

Music. It comes and goes. Don't try and hold it.
Wilhelmina Wiggins Fernandez as Cynthia Hawkins in **Diva** •336

Never burn bridges. Today's junior
prick, tomorrow's senior partner.
Sigourney Weaver as Katharine Parker in **Working Girl** •337

Bad table manners, my dear Gigi, have broken up more households than infidelity. *Isabel Jeans as Aunt Alicia in* **Gigi** •338

If you're going to kill someone, do it simply.
Cary Grant as Johnnie in **Suspicion** •339

It's best not to be too moral. You cheat yourself out of too much life.
Ruth Gordon as Maude in **Harold and Maude** •340

Your eyes are full of hate, 41. That's good. Hate keeps a man alive.
Jack Hawkins as Quintus Arrius in **Ben Hur** •341

You'll meet someone special. Someone who won't press charges.
Raoul Julia as Gomez in **Addams Family Values** •342

Lawyers should never marry other lawyers. This is called in-breeding; from this comes idiot children... and other lawyers.
David Wayne as Kip Lurie in **Adam's Rib** •343

Listen to the woman very carefully. Women know shit. I mean, even if you don't get the words, even if you don't know what the hell she's talking about, just listen.
Wesley Snipes as Sidney Deane in **White Men Can't Jump** •344

One should never, ever, interrupt one's desire to defecate.
I have inquired at the Bronx and London Zoos as to the daily bowel evacuations of primates. It is not once, twice, or three times, sir, but four. At the end of an average day, their cages
are filled with a veritable mountain of natural health.
Anthony Hopkins as Dr Kellogg in **The Road To Wellville** •345

Some day you'll learn that greatness is only the seizing of opportunity — clutching with your bare hands 'til the knuckles show white.
Mickey Rooney as Mi Taylor in **National Velvet** •346

Remember my dear, they only want one thing. Maybe they want it more than once, but it's still only one thing.
Judith Ivey as Celine's mum in **A Life Less Ordinary** •347

I never "faced facts" in life, so I survived. If I'd faced facts, I would have realised that I was a plain little girl with bow legs from Quincy, Massachusetts, and never gone on the stage. You must never face facts. *Ruth Gordon* •348

Don't confide in your girlfriends… if you let them advise you, they'll see to it in the name of friendship that you lose your husband and your home. I'm an old woman, my dear. I know my sex. *Lucille Watson as Mrs Moorehead in* **The Women** •349

Maybe it'll stop you trying to be so desperate about making more money than you can ever use. You can't take it with you, Mr Kirby. So what good is it? As near as I can see, the only thing you can take with you is the love of your friends.
Lionel Barrymore as Martin Vanderhoff in **You Can't Take It With You** •350

Charlotte: I just don't know what I'm supposed to be.
Bob: You'll figure that out. The more you know who you are, and what you want, the less you let things upset you.

Scarlett Johansson and Bill Murray in **Lost In Translation** •351

I believe God made me for a purpose.
But he also made me fast. When I run,
I feel His pleasure. *Ian Charleson as Eric Liddell
in* **Chariots of Fire** •352

The good news is you're gonna get the shot at the title.
The bad news is they want you to do the old flip-flop for 'em.
Joe Pesci as Joey to De Niro as Jake LaMotta in **Raging Bull** •353

Sports make you grunt and smell. Stay in school,
use your brains. Be a thinker not a stinker.

Carl Weathers as Apollo Creed in **Rocky** •354

Jack Lemmon is not one of those actors
will bore you to death discussing acting.
He'd rather bore you to death discussing golf.
George Cukor •355

Mother, just because I wear trackies and play sports does
not make me a lesbian! *Keira Knightley as Jules in* **Bend It Like Beckham** •356

93

Baseball's better than life. It's fair.

Robert De Niro as sick fan, Gil, in **The Fan** •357

It's the only game where a black man can wave a stick at a white man without starting a riot. *Gene Hackman as Rupert Anderson in* **Mississippi Burning** •358

There's no crying in baseball.

Tom Hanks as Coach Dugan in **A League of Their Own** •359

I try to learn your ways, understand your obsessions. But this baseball, it's so bleedin' boring, isn't it?

Christopher Eccleston as Raymond Calitri in **Gone In Sixty Seconds** •360

Thomas O'Malley: Why, your eyes are like sapphires sparkling so bright. They make the morning radiant and light.

Duchess: Oh, c'est tres jolie, monsieur. Very poetic. But it is not quite Shakespeare.

O'Malley: 'Course not. That's pure O'Malley, baby. Right off the cuff. Yeah. I got a million of 'em. *The voices of Phil Harris and Eva Gabor in* **The Aristocats** •361

This is very unusual. I've never been alone with a man before – even with my dress on. With my dress off, it is most unusual.

Audrey Hepburn as Princess Anne (not that one!) in **Roman Holiday** •362

Fran: Why can't I ever fall in love with someone nice, like you?

Baxter: Yeah, well, that's the way it crumbles, cookie-wise.

Shirley MacLaine and Jack Lemmon in **The Apartment** •363

You see? That is just like you, Harry. You say things like that, and you make it impossible for me to hate you. *Meg Ryan as Sally in* **When Harry Met Sally** •364

Virginia: I gotta warn ya, every man I've ever gone out with has been ruined.

Bugsy: Well that's what they get for messin' with my girl.

Warren Beatty as Bugsy Siegel goes for a cheeky precog line to Annette Bening in **Bugsy** •365

Oh, I can tell a lot about a man by dancing with him.
You know, some boys, well, when they take a girl in their arms
to dance, they, well, they make her feel sort of uncomfortable.
But with you, I had the feeling you know exactly what you
are doing and I could follow you every step of the way.
Kim Nowak as Madge in **Picnic** •366

Penny Lane: How old are you?
William Miller: Eighteen.
Penny: Me too! How old are we really?
William: Seventeen.
Penny: Me too!
William: Actually, I'm sixteen.
Penny: Me too. Isn't it funny?
The truth just sounds different.
William: I'm fifteen. *Kate Hudson and Patrick*
Fugit in **Almost Famous** •368

Mia: Are you a Bewitched
man or a Jeannie man?
Vincent: Bewitched, all the
way, though I always dug how
Jeannie always called Larry
Hagman "master".

Uma Thurman and John Travolta
make small talk in **Pulp Fiction**
•367

Listen, Ange, I've been looking for a girl every
Saturday night of my life. I'm thirty four years
old, and I'm tired of looking, that's all.
Ernest Borgnine as Marty Piletti in **Marty** •369

I sit here swooning with love and then suddenly you ask me a question and I don't like you any more. Do you have to sit there smiling at me like some smug, know-it-all schoolteacher?

Gregory Peck as Edwardes in **Spellbound** •370

Mr Allen, this may come as a shock to you, but there are some men who don't end every sentence with a proposition. *Doris Day as Jan Morrow in* **Pillow Talk** •371

If I wanted a man in my life I wouldn't have bought a VCR. *Michelle Pfeiffer in* **Frankie and Johnny** •372

Have you ever let a romantic moment make you do something that you knew was stupid?

Helen Hunt as Carol in **As Good As It Gets** •373

Joe: Look, you're a nice girl, but in case you're thinking of mothering me, forget it! I'm no stray dog you can pick up, and I like my neck without a collar. Now get lost!
Helen: Now I'm supposed to be hurt. Maybe even cry. But I won't. I think you're in trouble, and I'm going to help you.

John Payne and Coleen Gray in **Kansas City Confidential** •374

I don't bite, you know — unless it's called for.

Audrey Hepburn as Regina, flirts with Peter (Cary Grant) in **Charade** •375

Arthur: What do you do in the week, Doreen, do you ever go t' pictures?
Doreen: Only on Wednesday, why?
Arthur: That's funny, I go on Wednesday 'n' all. Which one d'you go to?
Doreen: The Grimley Hall
Arthur: I'll see you next Wednesday then, at seven.
Doreen: Fast worker aren't you? All right then, but not on the back row. *Albert Finney and Shirley Anne Field in* **Saturday Night and Sunday Morning** •376

When you first entered the restaurant, I thought you were handsome… and then, of course, you spoke. *Helen Hunt as Carol in* **As Good As It Gets** •377

Now it isn't that I don't like you, Susan, because, after all, in moments of quiet, I'm strangely drawn toward you, but — well, there haven't been any quiet moments. *Cary Grant as David in* **Bringing Up Baby** •378

Things are a little different now. First, you have to be friends. You have to like each other. Then, you neck. This could go on for years. Then you have tests, and then you get to do it with a condom. The good news is – you split the check. *Rob Reiner as Jay to Tom Hanks in* **Sleepless In Seattle** •379

I always just hoped that I'd meet some nice friendly girl, like the look of her, hope the look of me didn't make her physically sick, then pop the question and settle down and be happy. It worked for my parents. Well, apart from the divorce and all that.
James Fleet as Tom in **Four Weddings And A Funeral** •380

Mother, I do not need a blind date. Particularly not with some verbally incontinent spinster who drinks like a fish, smokes like a chimney and dresses like her mother. *Colin Firth as Mark Darcy in* **Bridget Jones' Diary** •381

Natalie: Hello, David. I mean "sir". Shit, I can't believe I've just said that. Oh and now I've gone and said "shit" – twice. I'm so sorry, sir.
P.M.: It's fine, it's fine. You could've said "fuck", and then we'd have been in real trouble.
Natalie: Thank you, sir. I did have an awful premonition that I was going to fuck up the first day. Oh piss-it!
Martine McCutcheon and Hugh Grant in **Love, Actually** •382

I don't think you're an idiot at all. I mean, there are elements of the ridiculous about you. Your mother's pretty interesting. And you really are an appallingly bad public speaker. And, er, you tend to let whatever's in your head come out of your mouth without much consideration of the consequences… But the thing is, er, what I'm trying to say, very inarticulately, is that, er in fact, perhaps despite appearances, I like you, very much. Just as you are. *Colin Firth as Mark Darcy in* **Bridget Jones' Diary** •383

You do have your moments. Not many of them, but you do have them.
Carrie Fisher as Princess Leia in **The Empire Strikes Back** •384

Spider-Man: You have a knack for getting into trouble.
Mary-Jane: You have a knack for saving my life.
I think I have a superhero stalker.
Spider-Man: I was in the neighborhood.
Tobey Maguire and Kirsten Dunst in **Spider-Man** •385

Jocelyn: I dream of poetry, speak poetry to me.
William: Your breasts… are beneath your throat.
Shannyn Sossamon and Heath Ledger in **A Knight's Tale** •386

101

It's not like I'm a lesbian or anything. It's just that all the people I've ever been attracted to happen to be girls. *Jessica Campbell as* **Tammy** *in* **Election** •387

Since you like chicks, right, do you just look at yourself naked in the mirror all the time? *Jason Lee as Banky in* **Chasing Amy**, *not quite getting to grips with lesbianism* •388

That is a babe! She makes me feel kinda funny, like when we used to climb the rope in gym-class. *Dana Carvey as Garth in* **Wayne's World** •389

It's the same old story. Boy finds girl, boy loses girl, girl finds boy, boy forgets girl, boy remembers girl, girl dies in a tragic blimp accident over the Orange Bowl on New Year's Day.

Leslie Nielsen as Frank Drebin in **Naked Gun** •390

Take off your clothes.

Repeated refrain of Daniel Day-Lewis as Tomas in **The Unbearable Lightness of Being** •391

Paul: May I smoke?

Sarah: No, but you can stay the night if you want.

Colin Firth and Ruth Gemmell in **Fever Pitch** •392

How about coming up to my place for a spot of heavy breathing? *Walter Matthau to Carol Burnett in* **Pete 'n' Tillie** •393

Charlie: I had a great time tonight and I'd really love to kiss you, but I think that if I kiss you we'll end up kissing on the couch and if we end up kissing on the couch then chances are we'll kiss in the bedroom and if we kiss in the bedroom then, you know, that's the part I always rush into and I just don't think it's a good idea to rush into spending the night together.

Harriet: I wanna spend the night together.

Charlie: I have no problem with that.

Mike Myers and Nancy Travis in **So I Married An Axe Murderer** •394

Eric: Maybe we could have dinner…
Gracie: What do you mean? Like a date?
Eric: No! Just casual dinner… If we happen to
have sex afterwards so be it!
Ben Bratt and Sandra Bullock in **Miss Congeniality** •395

I'd like to see you with your pants off, Mr Reed.

Diane Keaton as Louise Bryant, to Warren Beatty in **Reds** •396

Of course I may bring a boyfriend home occasionally,
but only occasionally, because I do think that one ought
to go to the man's room if one can. I mean,
it doesn't look so much as if one expected it, does it?
Liza Minelli as Sally Bowles in **Cabaret** •397

Robert Danvers: If I made a pass at you now, what would your reaction be? Marion: You want the result before you place the bet? *Peter Sellers and Goldie Hawn in* **There's A Girl In My Soup** •398

Take me to bed or lose me forever.

Carole (Meg Ryan) spells it out in **Top Gun** •399

If you take my heart by surprise, the rest of my body has the right to follow. *Albert Finney as* **Tom Jones** •400

Listen, sugar, the only way that you can keep me warm is to wrap me up in a marriage license.

Gloria Grahame as Angel in **The Greatest Show On Earth** •401

All they have to do is play eight bars of *"Come to Me, My Melancholy Baby"*, and my spine turns to custard. I get goose pimply all over and I come to 'em.

Marilyn Monroe in **Some Like It Hot** •402

I mean, any gentleman with the slightest chic would give a girl $50 for the powder room. And hold out for the cab fare, too. That's another fifty.

Audrey Hepburn as Holly Golightly in **Breakfast at Tiffany's** •403

Come on, darling. Why don't you kick off your spurs?
Elizabeth Taylor as Leslie in **Giant** •404

Guess I'm not used to sleeping nights anyway.
Jean Harlow as Vantine, complaining about the heat(?) in **Red Dust** •405

If you really want to see fireworks, it's better with the lights off.
Grace Kelly as Frances in **To Catch A Thief** •406

It's going to be a long night.
And I don't like the book I started.
Eva Marie Saint as Eve in **North By Northwest** •407

Preview of coming attractions.
Grace Kelly, holding up a negligee, as Lisa in **Rear Window** •408

There are only two things to do around here. You got a TV? No?
Well, you're now down to one. *Virginia Madsen as Dolly Harshaw in*
The Hot Spot •409

What d'you do, boy-scout, lose your compass?

Gloria Grahame as Angel to Cornel Wilde, when he mistakenly enters the ladies' room in **The Greatest Show On Earth** •410

Joe: I always have liked redheads.
Cassie: You shouldn't. Red means stop.
Joe: I'm colour blind.

George Raft and Ann Sheridan in **They Drive By Night** •411

Would you be shocked if I put on something more comfortable?

Jean Harlow as Helen in **Hell's Angels** •412

You know how to whistle, don't you, Steve?
You just put your lips together, and blow.

Lauren Bacall in **To Have and Have Not** •413

Tracy: You know, it's legal for me to take you down to the station, and sweat it out of you under the lights.
Mahoney: I sweat a lot better in the dark.

Warren Beatty and Madonna in **Dick Tracy** •414

Go on, you can hold my hand, I won't blackmail you for it afterwards. *Ingrid Bergman as Alicia in* **Notorious** •415

Roberta: If there's one thing I have a weakness for, it's champagne.
Ed: If there's one thing I have a weakness for, it's girls who have a weakness.
Marilyn Monroe and Jack Paar in **Love Nest** •416

Tell me, how does a girl like you get to be a girl like you? *Cary Grant as Roger Thornhill in* **North By Northwest** •417

The moment I saw you, I had an idea you had an idea.
Claudette Colbert as Eve Peabody in **Midnight** •418

Can I get ya anything? Coffee? Tea? Me?
Joan Cusack as Cynthia in **Working Girl** •419

Why don't I get someone else to watch the sheep for me tonight?
Annie Potts (voice) as Bo Peep, gives Woody the come-on in **Toy Story** •420

I am flattered that a midnight visit from the wolf should prove so exciting to a lamb of your coolness and self-possession. *Cedric Hardwicke as the Marquis of Steyne in* **Becky Sharp** •421

I find you very attractive. Your assertiveness tells me that you feel the same way about me. But ritual remains that we must do a series of platonic actions before we can have intercourse. But all I really want to do is have sex with you as soon as possible.
Russell Crowe as John Nash delivers one of the more articulate movie come-ons •422

Craig: Can I buy you a drink, Maxine.
Maxine: Are you married?
Craig: Yes, but enough about me.
John Cusack and Catherine Keener in **Being John Malkovich** •423

Oh, I guess this isn't the bathroom, is it?
Anne Bancroft barges in on Dustin Hoffman in **The Graduate** •424

Oh no, Mrs Robinson, I think you're the most attractive of all my parents' friends, I mean that.
Dustin Hoffman as Benjamin Braddock in **The Graduate** •425

Mrs Robinson, you're trying to seduce me, aren't you?

Dustin Hoffman again, as the penny drops in **The Graduate** •426

Wanna dance, or would you rather just suck face?

Henry Fonda to Katharine Hepburn in **On Golden Pond** •427

When I see two people on the screen kiss with their mouths open, I don't like to watch. It seems too personal for me.
Henry Fonda •428

Learn your lines, don't bump into furniture and in kissing scenes, keep your mouth closed.

Ronald Reagan •429

Robert Redford's the very best kisser I ever met.
Meryl Streep •430

In Westerns you were permitted to kiss your horse but never your girl.

Gary Cooper •431

110

Lucy: What are you doing?
Harry: Nothing, I'm just getting some lint off you.
Drew Barrymore and Adam Sandler share an oft-to-be-repeated first kiss in **50 First Dates** •432

I'd love to kiss you but I just washed my hair.
Bette Davis as Madge in **Cabin In the Cotton** •433

I'd rather kiss a tarantula.

Gene Kelly as Lockwood on Jean Hagen as Lina in **Singin' In The Rain** •434

Daniel: OK, tell me more about practicing French kissing with the girls at school.
Bridget: It wasn't French kissing!
Daniel: Don't care – make it up!
Hugh Grant and Renee Zellweger in **Bridget Jones' Diary** •436

I don't know how to kiss, or I would kiss you. Where do the noses go?
Ingrid Bergman to Gary Cooper in **For Whom the Bell Tolls** •435

Skylar: You were hoping for a goodnight kiss?

Will: No. You know, I'll tell ya, I was hoping to get goodnight laid.

Minnie Driver and Matt Damon see things differrently in **Good Will Hunting** •437

Oh, Frank, my lips are hot. Kiss my hot lips. *Sara Kellerman earns her nickname in* M*A*S*H •438

Kiss me, Mike. I want you to kiss me. Kiss me. The liar's kiss that says I love you and means something else.

Gaby Rodgers as Lily Carver in **Kiss Me Deadly** •439

I'm gonna show you what yum-yum is. Here's yum. Here's the other yum. And here's yum-yum.

Barbara Stanwyck as Sugarpuss in **Ball of Fire** •440

Julian: I think I'm going to kiss you. Stephanie: When will you know for sure?

Walter Matthau and Ingrid Bergman in **Cactus Flower** •441

You should be kissed, and often, by someone who knows how.
Clark Gable as Rhett Butler in **Gone With The Wind** •442

Never mind about loving me. You're a woman who is sending a soldier to his death with a beautiful memory. Scarlett, kiss me. Kiss me, once.
Clark Gable as Rhett Butler in **Gone With The Wind** •443

Not only did I enjoy that kiss last night, I was awed by the efficiency behind it.
Cary Grant as John Robie in **To Catch A Thief** •444

Joe: I think you're on the right track.
Sugar Cane: I must be. Your glasses are beginning to steam up.
Tony Curtis and Marilyn Monroe in **Some Like It Hot** •445

Joe: It's like smoking without inhaling. Sugar Cane: So inhale.

Tony Curtis and Marilyn Monroe in **Some Like It Hot** •446

That thing, that moment, when you kiss someone and everything around becomes hazy and the only thing in focus is you and this person and you realize that that person is the only person that you're supposed to kiss for the rest of your life, and for one moment you get this amazing gift and you want to laugh and you want to cry because you feel so lucky that you found it and so scared that it will go away all at the same time.

Drew Barrymore as Josie in **Never Been Kissed** •447

I think we might begin with one or two Latin terms.
John Malkovich as Valmont seducing Uma Thurman **In Dangerous Liaisons** •448

COMPLETE NUDITY IS NEVER PERMITTED. THIS INCLUDES NUDITY IN FACT OR IN SILHOUETTE, OR ANY LECHEROUS OR LICENTIOUS NOTICE THEREOF BY OTHER CHARACTERS IN THE PICTURE.

from The Hays Code, the rules governing morality in the movies for over thirty years •449

There's no mystery, no privacy. And frankly, no sex, either… a suggestion of sex is much more interesting than actually showing it, don't you think? *Myrna Loy* •450

In love scenes on beds you had to keep one foot on the floor at all times, which made it rather like playing snooker or pool. *Albert Finney (attrib)* •451

115

They are doing things on the screen these days that the French don't even put on postcards. *Bob Hope* •452

America is so puritanical and hypocritical and it seems that anything to do with sex is taboo. Should I pretend that I'm scandalised about playing a prostitute or pretend that 224 million Americans don't have orgasms? Good sex belongs in the cinema just as much as a good gag. *Kathleen Turner* •453

If they didn't show it on the screen, most people would never know about oral sex.

Mary Whitehouse. Speak for yourself, Lady. •454

Acting is like sex. You should do it, not talk about it.

Joanne Woodward •455

I always think that sex is much healthier than violence.

Otto Preminger •456

Now, just because someone sees, you know, two naked people asleep in bed together, it doesn't necessarily prove sex was involved. It does, however, make for a very strong case.

Toni Collette as Mandy in **Velvet Goldmine** •457

Hannah: Mom caught me and Jules
in the pool together?
Ginger: So?
Hannah: We weren't swimming.

*Erika Christensen and Eva Amurri as Susan Sarandon's
daughters in* **The Banger Sisters** •458

Lavinia: You don't think maybe they
were just skinny-dipping?
Suzette: No, they were going at it.
Lavinia: You don't think maybe they
were just rubbing up against each other?
Suzette: No, they were fucking.

*Susan Sarandon and Goldie Hawn
as* **The Banger Sisters** •459

Julie: He told me he loved me.
Helen: Oh, sweetie. They say that – then they come.

Martha Plimpton & Dianne Wiest in **Parenthood** •460

Vicky: I want it to be the right time, the right place...
Jessica: It's not a space shuttle launch, it's sex.

Tara Reid and Natasha Lyonne in **American Pie** •461

Romy: You have absolutely no proof
that you're cuter.
Michele: Oh, proof. You want proof?
Ok, fine. Who lost their virginity first?
Romy:Oh, big wow, with your cousin
Barry. I wouldn't brag about it.

Mira Sorvino and Lisa Kudrow in **Romy and
Michele's High School Reunion** •462

I'm so proud of you. You finally got laid properly. *Susan
Sarandon as Louise to Geena Davis in* **Thelma and Louise** •463

She was astonishing. So much so that I ended by falling on my
knees and pledging her eternal love. And do you know that at that
time and for several hours afterwards, I actually meant it.

John Malkovich as Valmont in **Dangerous Liaisons** •464

Women need a reason to have sex.
Men just need a place.

Billy Crystal as Mitch in **City Slickers** •465

Shall we shag now, or shall we shag later? How do you like to do it?
Do you like to wash up first? You know, top and tails? Whore's bath?
Personally, before I'm on the job, I like to give my undercarriage a
bit of a how's your father! *The Austin Powers touch* •466

Sally: Well, do you sleep with girls or don't you?
Brian: Sally, you don't ask questions like that.
Sally: I do.
Liza Minelli and Michael York in **Cabaret** •467

You better run me back to the hotel.
You got me hotter than Georgia asphalt.
Laura Dern as Lula in **Wild At Heart** •468

Have you ever done it in an elevator?
Glenn Close as Alex to Michael Douglas in **Fatal Attraction** •469

Have you ever fucked on cocaine, Nick? It's nice.
Sharon Stone, shortly before uncrossing her legs in **Basic Instinct** •470

My God. I haven't been fucked like that since grade school.

Helena Bonham-Carter as Marla in **Fight Club** •471

So, do you want more eggs or should we just fuck on the linoleum one last time?

Meryl Streep as Francesca in **The Bridges of Madison County** •472

And the first thing that flashed into my gulliver was that I'd like to have her right down there on the floor with the old in-out, real savage.

Malcolm McDowell as Alex in **A Clockwork Orange** •473

"Well, I believe in the soul, the cock, the pussy, the small of a woman's back, the hanging curve ball, high fiber, good scotch, that the novels of Susan Sontag are self-indulgent, overrated crap. I believe Lee Harvey Oswald acted alone. I believe there ought to be a constitutional amendment outlawing Astroturf and the designated hitter. I believe in the sweet spot, soft-core pornography, opening your presents Christmas morning rather than Christmas Eve and I believe in long, slow, deep, soft, wet kisses that last three days.

Crash (Kevin Costner) smooth talks Annie (Susan Sarandon) in **Bull Durham** *(1988)* •474

Fire walk with me.

Sheryl Lee as Laura Palmer in **Twin Peaks** •475

Catherine: What do we do now, Nick?
Nick: Fuck like minxs, raise rugrats, live happily ever after.
Catherine: Hate rugrats.
Nick: Fuck like minxs, forget rugrats, and live happily ever after.

Nick Curran (Michael Douglas) shows tenacity with
Catherine Trammell (Sharon Stone) in **Basic Instinct** •476

Luisa: You have to make the clitoris your best friend.
Tenoch: What kind of friend is always hiding?

Maribel Verdu and Diego Luna in **Y Tu Mama Tambien** •477

Jessica: You've never had an orgasm? Not even manually?
Vicky: I've never tried it.
Jessica: You've never double-clicked your mouse?

Natasha Lyonne and Tara Reid in **American Pie** •478

Oh, all right! So shoot me, I was whacking off! That's right,
I was choking the bishop, chafing the carrot, you know, saying
"hi" to my monster! *Kevin Spacey as Lester Burnham in* **American Beauty** •479

I don't know what I am, darling. I've tried several varieties of sex.
The conventional position makes me claustrophobic, and the others
give me either a stiff neck or lockjaw. *Tallulah Bankhead* •480

I've played so many hookers they don't
pay me in the regular way any more.
They leave it on the dresser.
Shirley MacLaine •481

Working in Hollywood does give one a
certain expertise in the field of prostitution.
Jane Fonda •482

Men have paid $200 for me, and here you are, turning down
a freebie. You could get a perfectly good dishwasher for that.
Jane Fonda as Bree Daniels in **Klute** •483

I'll do fag tricks. I'll do kinks.
I'll do anything you want me to do.
Richard Gere as Julian Kaye in **American Gigolo** •484

The two things I love most in life are sex and money. It's just
that I didn't know until much later that they were connected.
Ellen McElduff in **Working Girls** •485

122

I appreciate this whole seduction thing you got
going, but let me give you a tip: I'm a sure thing.
Julia Roberts' tart with a heart in **Pretty Woman** •486

Mamma, face it! I was the slut of all time.
Elizabeth Taylor as Gloria Wandrous in **Butterfield 8** •487

It's just like a tupperware party really,
but I sell sex instead of plastic containers.
Julie Walters as Cynthia Payne in **Personal Services** •488

Deep down I'm a sensitive and vulnerable girl.
Don't let my dildos, vibrators and handcuffs fool you.
Andrea Naschak (aka porn star April Rayne) as Sabra in
Hold Me, Thrill Me, Kiss Me •489

You know, it's always a business doing pleasure with you, Charlie!

Dolly Parton as Miss Mona in **The Best Little Whorehouse In Texas** •490

You boys gotta make up your minds if you want to get your cookies. Cause if you want to get your cookies, I've got girls up here that'll do more tricks than a goddamn monkey on a hundred yards of grapevine.

Warren Beatty as John McCabe in **McCabe and Mrs Miller** •491

There are girls your age that are just like me. We are the guiltless pleasures of the lonely human being. You won't get us pregnant or have us to supper with mommy and daddy. We work under you, we work on you and we work for you. Man made us better at what we do than was ever humanly possible. *Jude Law as Gigolo Joe in* A.I. •492

I'm not the sort of person men marry.
Joan Fontaine as Mrs De Winter in **Rebecca** •493

I was born to be married. I just so happen to come from a long line of married people. My mom and dad, they were married. Their moms and dads, they were married, too. *Tom Hanks as Allen Bauer in* **Splash!** •494

When I married Miles, we were both a couple of maladjusted misfits. We are still maladjusted misfits, and we have loved every minute of it. *Thelma Ritter as Stella in* **Rear Window** •495

I've no regrets. I've been everywhere and done everything. I've eaten caviar at Cannes, sausage rolls at the dogs. I've played baccarat at Biarritz, and darts with a rural dean. What is there left for me but marriage? *Margaret Lockwood as Iris Henderson in* **The Lady Vanishes** •496

Mattie: Why did you two ever get married?
Carolyn: Oh, I don't know. It was raining and we were in Pittsburgh. *Helen Broderick and Barbara Stanwyck in* **The Bride Walks Out** •497

Rosalind: Ambrose seems to think of only two things; that silly old car and the other thing.
Wendy: What other thing? Oh, no! My husband only thinks about the car. *Kay Kendall and Dinah Sheridan in* **Genevieve** •498

You're like an old coat that is hanging in his closet. Every time he reaches in, there you are. Don't be there once.

Joan Blondell, as Peg Costello, to Katharine Hepburn, as Bunny Watson, in **Desk Set** •499

Pete: My plumber tells me that the pursuit of women is flight from women.
Tillie: What does that mean?
Pete: How the hell do I know? Am I a plumber?
Walter Matthau and Carol Burnett in **Pete 'n' Tillie** •500

There'll be no locks or bolts between us, Mary-Kate – except for those in your own mercenary little heart.
John Wayne as Red Will Danaher, to Maureen O'Hara in **The Quiet Man** •501

Frida Kahlo: What do you think matters most for a good marriage?

Guillermo Kahlo: A short memory.

Frida: Why did you get married?

Guillermo: I can't remember.
Salma Hayek and Roger Rees in **Frida** •502

Marriage is like a dull meal with the dessert at the beginning.

Jose Ferrer as Toulouse-Lautrec in **Moulin Rouge** •503

Marriage is like the Middle East. There is no solution.
Pauline Collins as **Shirley Valentine** •504

More good women have been lost to marriage than war, famine and disease.
Glenn Close as Cruella de Vil in **101 Dalmatians** •505

I don't get married again because I can't find anyone I dislike enough to inflict that kind of torture on.

Roy Scheider as Joe Gideon in **All That Jazz** •506

The girl: You really can't get a divorce?
Sullivan: You can't get a divorce without collusion and she won't collude.

Veronica Lake and Joel McCrae in **Sullivan's Travels** •507

Fairbanks: Say, are you two still married or what?
I find it all very confusing.
Chaplin: It's not at all confusing. You see, when everyone thought we were having an affair, we were married. Now that everyone realizes we're married, we're getting divorced.
Fairbanks: Man's a wizard with women. No question about it.

Kevin Kilne and Robert Downey jnr in **Chaplin** •508

Actors marrying actors play a dangerous game. They're always fighting over the mirror. *Burt Reynolds* •509

Marriage requires a special talent, like acting, like writing. I haven't got the talent, so I don't marry. And monogamy requires genius.

Warren Beatty. •510

I dunno what to tell you, Marge! I don't think about things.
I mean, I respect those who do, but... I just try and make the day not hurt until I can crawl back in with you.

Homer Simpson in **The Simpsons Movie** •511

128

Barbara Stanwyck is my favourite. My God, I could just sit and dream of being married to her, having a little cottage out in in the hills, vines round the door. I'd come home from the office tired and weary, and I'd be met by Barbara, walking through the door holding an apple pie she'd cooked herself. And wearing no underwear. *Billy Wilder* •512

Chains don't hold a marriage together. It's threads, hundreds of tiny threads which sew people together through the years. That's what makes a marriage last; more than passion, or even sex.

Simone Signoret •513

Above all things I believe in love!
Love is like oxygen. Love is a
many-splendoured thing. Love
lifts us up where we belong.
All you need is love!
Ewan McGregor as Christian in **Moulin Rouge** •514

I wanted to marry her when I saw the moonlight
shining on the barrel of her father's shotgun.
Eddie Albert as Ali Hakim in **Oklahoma!** •515

Leia: Han, I love you.
Han Solo: (about to be deep-frozen) I know.
Carrie Fisher and Harrison Ford in **The Empire Strikes Back** •516

I do. 'Til you and I die, and die,
and die again. 'Til death us do part.

Juliette Lewis as Mallory in **Natural Born Killers** •517

Look at her. I would die for her. I would
kill for her. Either way, what bliss.
Raoul Julia as Gomez in **Addams Family Values** •518

Don't torture yourself, Gomez.
That's my job. *Anjelica Huston as Morticia in*
The Addams Family •519

Gomez, last night – you were unhinged. You were like some
desperate, howling demon. You frightened me. Do it again!
Anjelica Huston as Morticia in **The Addams Family** •520

In short, to recap it slightly in a clearer version, …the
words of David Cassidy in fact, …while he was still with
the Partridge family, …"I think I love you," and …I, I just
wondered by any chance you wouldn't like to… No, no, no
of course not… I'm an idiot, he's not.
Hugh Grant as Charles in **Four Weddings And A Funeral** •521

But for now, let me say – Without hope or agenda – Just because it's Christmas – And at Christmas you tell the truth – To me, you are perfect – And my wasted heart will love you – Until you look like this.

Andrew Lincoln as Mark, holding up storyboards outside Keira Knightley's window in **Love, Actually** •522

Nina: I really, truly, madly, deeply, passionately, remarkably, …deliciously love you.
Jamie: I really, truly, madly, passionately, remarkably, deliciously… juicily love you.
Nina: Deeply! Deeply! You passed on deeply, which was your word, which means you couldn't have meant it! So you're a fraud, that's it! *Juliet Stevenson and Alan Rickman in* **Truly, Madly, Deeply** •524

When you fall in love, it is a temporary madness. It erupts like an earthquake, and then it subsides. And when it subsides, you have to make a decision. You have to work out whether your roots are become so entwined together that it is inconceivable that you should ever part. Because this is what love is.
John Hurt as Iannis in **Captain Corelli's Mandolin** •523

So it's not gonna be easy. It's gonna be really hard. We're gonna have to work at this every day, but I want to do that because I want you. I want all of you, for ever, you and me, every day.

Ryan Gosling as Noah to Rachel McAdams as Allie in **The Notebook** •525

132

Inman: This doesn't come out right. If it were enough to stand, without the words.
Ada: It is. It is.
Inman: Look at the sky now. What color is it? Or the way a hawk flies. Or you wake up and your ribs are bruised thinking so hard on somebody. What do you call that?
Jude Law and Nicole Kidman in **Cold Mountain** •526

There are only four questions of value in life, Don Octavio. What is sacred? Of what is the spirit made? What is worth living for? and What is worth dying for? The answer to each is the same: only love. *Johnny Depp as Don Juan De Marco* •527

I'm in love with you. I love you. I am totally, completely mad for you. My heart stops every time I look at you. Personally, I think we should be married. I definitely want to have kids – four or five, if possible. There, I said it. It wasn't so difficult. You don't have to say anything. That's fine with me. I just wanted to get it out, myself. Talk about a load off.
Al Pacino **in Frankie and Johnny** •528

Hanging would be a small price to pay for the company of such a charming lady.
Errol Flynn as **Robin Hood** •529

Oh, Fred, I've been so foolish. I've fallen in love. I'm an ordinary woman, I didn't think such things could happen to ordinary people.

Celia Johnson as Laura Jesson in **Brief Encounter** •530

You can't hurt me. Westley and I are joined by the bonds of love. And you cannot track that, not with a thousand bloodhounds, and you cannot break it, not with a thousand swords.

Robin Wright as Buttercup in **The Princess Bride** •531

I might be the only person on the face of the earth that knows you're the greatest woman on earth. I might be the only one who appreciates how amazing you are in every single thing that you do, and how you are with Spencer, "Spence," and in every single thought that you have, and how you say what you mean, and how you almost always mean something that's all about being straight and good. I think most people miss that about you, and I watch them, wondering how they can watch you bring their food, and clear their tables and never get that they just met the greatest woman alive. And the fact that I get it makes me feel good, about me. *Jack Nicholson as Melvin Udall in* **As Good As It Gets** •532

134

Sgt Milton Warden: I've never been so miserable in my life as I have since I met you.
Karen: Neither have I.
Warden: I wouldn't trade a minute of it.
Karen: Neither would I.
Burt Lancaster and Deborah Kerr in
From Here to Eternity •533

I love you. You're my only reason to stay alive ... if that's what I am.

Robert Pattinson as Edward in
Twilight : New Moon •535

How can you change one's entire life and build a new one in one moment of love? And yet that's what you make me want to close my eyes and do. *Greta Garbo as Marguerite Gauthier in* **Camille** •534

But love don't make things nice. It ruins everything. It breaks your heart. It makes things a mess. We aren't here to make things perfect. The snowflake is perfect, the stars are perfect, not us. Not us. We are here to ruin ourselves and to break our hearts and love the wrong people and die. *Nicolas Cage as Ronny in* **Moonstruck** •536

I don't owe a nickel in this town. I will eat anything that's put down in front of me. I can fix anything electrical. I'm all right after my first cup of coffee — I want that bad, though. I got me a new job at the gas station, and I turn my paycheck over the minute I get it – that's every Friday. And I come straight home from work, and I stay there. I got me and Alice. We're alone. You got your two kids. You're alone. If you could help me, maybe I could help you. *Beau Bridges as Sonny in* **Norma Rae** •537

I love him because he's the kind of guy that gets drunk on a glass of buttermilk, and I love the way he blushes right up over his ears. I love him because he doesn't know how to kiss, the jerk! I love him, Joe.
Barbara Stanwyck as Sugarpuss in **Ball of Fire** •538

I don't want to live forever if you're not going to be with me.
Hume Cronyn as Joe to Jessica Tandy in **Cocoon** •539

I don't want to waste another
moment of my life without you in it.
Zach Braff as Andrew Largeman in **Garden State** •540

Lewis: Will you marry this foolish, frightened old man who needs you more than he can bear to say, and loves you even though he hardly knows how?
Joy: Just this once.
Anthony Hopkins and Debra Winger in **Shadowlands** •541

Oh, Jerry, don't let's ask for the moon. We have the stars.
Bette Davis as Charlotte Vale in **Now, Voyager** •542

Viola: (in disguise) Tell me how you love her, Will.
Shakespeare: Like a sickness and its cure together.
Gwyneth Paltrow and Joseph Fiennes in **Shakespeare In Love** •543

Edmund: Fanny, I've loved you my whole life.
Fanny: I know, Edmund.
Edmund: No! I've loved you as a man loves a woman.
As a hero loves a heroine. As I have never loved anyone.
Jonny Lee Miller and Frances O'Connor in **Mansfield Park** •544

Carson: I'm afraid I'm pretty crazy about you.
Barbara: Always? For keeps?
Carson: And after that, too.
Clark Gable and Mary Astor in **Red Dust** •545

I thought we would meet only in death.
Freida Pinto as Latika to Jamal (Dev Patel) in **Slumdog Millionaire** •546

Love is a fire. But whether it is going
to warm your heart or burn down
your house, you can never tell.
Joan Crawford •547

Lust. And respect. And forgiveness. And persistence.
Paul Newman on the strength of his marriage to Joanne Woodward •548

Alicia: Say it again, it keeps me awake.
Bruce: I love you. *Ingrid Bergman and Cary Grant in* **Notorious** •549

137

Stay alive, no matter what occurs. I will find you. No matter how long it takes, no matter how far. I will find you. *Daniel Day-Lewis as Hawkeye in* **The Last of the Mohicans.** •550

C'est tellement simple, l'amour.

Arletty as Garance in **Les Enfants du Paradis** •551

I swear, if you existed I'd divorce you.

Elizabeth Taylor in **Who's Afraid of Virginia Woolf** •552

Thank you, Daniel, that is very good to know. But if staying here means working within ten yards of you, frankly I'd rather have a job wiping Saddam Hussein's arse.

Bridget (Rene Zellweger) declines to acceptan apology from Daniel (Hugh Grant) in **Bridget Jones' Diary** •553

I'm loud, and I'm vulgar, and I wear the pants in the house because somebody's got to. But I am not a monster.

Elizabeth Taylor in **Who's Afraid of Virginia Woolf** •554

The only thing that we've got left in common is the same mattress.

Burt Lancaster as Mel Bakersfield, about his wife, in **Airport.** •555

No matter who you marry, you wake up married to someone else.

Marlon Brando as Sky Masterson in **Guys and Dolls** •556

I'm not living with you. We occupy the same cage, that's all. *Elizabeth Taylor as Maggie Pollitt in* **Cat on a Hot Tin Roof** •557

When men get around me, they get allergic to wedding rings. You know, "big sister type. Good old Ida. You can talk it over with her man-to-man." I'm getting awfully tired of men talking to me man-to-man.

Eve Arden as Ida in **Mildred Pierce** •558

Joe, do you have any idea what's available to a woman of 33? Married men. Drunks. Pretty boys looking for someone to support them. Lunatics looking for their fifth divorce! It's quite a list, isn't it? *Celeste Holm as Sylvia in* **The Tender Trap** •559

Truth is pain and sweat and paying bills and making love to a woman you don't love any more. Truth is dreams that don't come true and nobody prints your name in the paper until you die.
Burl Ives as Big Daddy in **Cat On A Hot Tin Roof** •560

A woman can do anything, get anywhere, as long as she doesn't fall in love.
Joan Crawford as Louise in **Possessed** •561

I'm not going to divorce you. I am going to forgive you. I am going to forget this ever happened. I'm going to figure out why it happened, and I'm never going to bring it up again as long as I live. And now, I'm going in there, and I'm going to spend every last cent you have.

Elaine May as Millie Michaels in **California Suite** •562

Our people once were warriors. But unlike you, Jake, they were people with mana, pride; people with spirit. If my spirit can survive living with you for eighteen years, then I can survive anything. *Rena Owen as Beth in* **Once Were Warriors** •563

Suzanne: You said you loved me.
Jack: I meant it at the time.
Suzanne: What is it, a viral love? Kind of a 24-hour thing?
Meryl Streep and Dennis Quaid in **Postcards From The Edge** •564

You are probably going to be a very successful computer person. But you're going to go through life thinking that girls don't like you because you're a nerd. And I want you to know, from the bottom of my heart, that that won't be true. It'll be because you're an asshole.
Rooney Mara as Erica breaks up with pre-facebook Mark Zuckerberg (Jesse Eisenberg) in **The Social Network** •565

You know what these small towns are like. Girl spends her entire time in high school looking for the guy she's going to marry, and spends the rest of her life trying to figure out why.

Gene Hackman as Rupert Anderson in **Mississippi Burning** •566

Mookie, the last time I trusted you, we ended up with a son.

Rosie Perez as Spike Lee's girl, Tina, in **Do The Right Thing** •567

Cal Hockley: Where are you going? To him?
To be a whore to a gutter rat?
Rose: I'd rather be his whore than your wife.

Billy Zane and Kate Winslet in **Titanic** •568

Cheetah, that bastard, bit me whenever he could.
The apes were all homosexuals, eager to wrap
their paws around Johnny Weismuller's thighs.
They were jealous of me, and I
loathed them. *Maureen O'Sullivan, a bitter Jane* •569

Brodie! I've always taken you with a grain of salt. On your birthday, when you told me to do a striptease to the theme of "Mighty Mouse", I said okay. On prom night at the hotel when you told me to sleep under the bed in case your mother burst in, I did it. And even during my grandmother's funeral when you told my relatives that you could see her nipples through her burial dress, I let that slide. But if you think I'm gonna suffer any of your shit with a smile now that we're broken up, you're in for some serious fucking disappointment.

Shannen Doherty as Rene in **Mallrats** •570

Adultery, sometimes necessary plot material, must not be explicitly treated, or justified, or presented attractively. *from The Hays Code, Hollywood's self-censorship rules for over thirty years.* •571

Make a married woman laugh and you're halfway there.

Michael Caine as **Alfie** •572

My understanding of women only goes as far as the pleasures. When it comes to the pain, I'm like every other bloke, I don't want to know.

Michael Caine in **Alfie** •573

Most men in this town think monogamy is a type of wood.

Peggy Brandt as Amy in **The Mask** •574

How dare he make love to me and not be a married man!

Ingrid Bergman as Anna Kalman in **Indiscreet** •575

Your idea of fidelity is not having more than one man in bed at the same time.

Dirk Bogarde to Julie Christie in **Darling** •576

You want monogamy, marry a swan.

Steven Hill as Harry in **Heartburn** •577

This is not an affair, it's a one-night stand that happened twice.

Anthony LaPaglia as Leon in **Lantana** •578

Husbands are chiefly good lovers when they are betraying their wives.

Marilyn Monroe •579

Why can't women play the game properly? Everyone knows that in love affairs only the man has the right to lie.

Clifton Webb as Shadwell in **Three Coins in the Fountain** •580

145

Matty: You're not too smart, are you? I like that in a man. •581

Ned: Can I buy you a drink?
Matty: I told you, I got a husband.
Ned: I'll buy him one, too.
Matty: He's out of town.
Ned: My favourite kind, we'll drink to him. •582

Ned: Maybe you shouldn't dress like that.
Matty: This is a blouse and a skirt. I don't know what you're talking about.
Ned: You shouldn't wear that body. •583

Matty: My temperature runs a little high.
Ned: Maybe you need a tune-up.
Matty: Don't tell me – you have just the right tool. •584

Kathleen Turner (Matty) and William Hurt (Ned) in **Body Heat**

French films follow a basic formula: Husband sleeps with Jeanne because Bernadette cuckolded him by sleeping with Christophe. In the end they all go off to a restaurant.

Sophie Marceau •585

To be with another woman, that is French. To be caught, that is American.

Anton Rodgers as Inspector Andre in **Dirty Rotten Scoundrels** •586

Tom had always thought that any woman was better than none, while Molly never felt that one man was quite as good as two.

Michael MacLiammoir narrating in **Tom Jones** •587

The first man that can think up a good explanation how he can be in love with his wife *and* another woman is going to win that prize they're always giving out in Sweden.

Mary Cecil as Maggie in **The Women** •588

You look pretty good without your shirt on, you know. The sight of that through the kitchen window made me put down my dish towel more than once.

Patricia Neal as Alma Brown to Paul Newman in **Hud** •589

When Arthur was having his little affair, every time he got on a plane I would imagine the plane crash, the funeral, what I would wear at the funeral. The flirting at the funeral. How soon I could start dating after the funeral.

Stockard Channing as Julie in **Heartburn** •590

You had a mistress – I forgave you. My sister has a lover – you drive her from the house. Why can you not be honest for once in your life, and say to yourself, what Helen has done, I have done.

Emma Thompson as Margaret Schlegel to Anthony Hopkins in **Howard's End** •591

JD Sheldrake: You see a girl a couple of times a week, just for laughs, and right away they think you're going to divorce your wife. Now I ask you, is that fair?

Bud Baxter: No sir, it's very unfair – especially to your wife.

Fred MacMurray and Jack Lemmon in **The Apartment** •592

Humbert: You know, I've missed you terribly.

Lolita: I haven't missed you. In fact, I've been revoltingly unfaithful to you.

James Mason and Sue Lyon in **Lolita** •593

A man doesn't tell a woman
what to do. She tells herself.

Cary Grant as T.R. Devlin in Hitchcock's **Notorious** •594

Doesn't it ever enter a man's head that a woman can do without him?

Ida Lupino in **Road House** •595

Bernie: Why is it that women always think
they understand men better than men do?
Georgie: Maybe because they live with them.

William Holden and Grace Kelly in **The Country Girl** •596

Valmont: Why do you suppose we only feel
compelled to chase the ones who run away?
Marquise de Merteuil: Immaturity?

John Malkovich and Glenn Close in **Dangerous Liaisons** •597

A woman needs security like a man needs approval.

Scott Wilson as Hale in **The Way of The Gun** •598

Cal: How about we say what we want on three? Ok …
Cal: Creme brulee!
Emily (simultaneously): I want a divorce.

Steve Carell and Julianne Moore in **Crazy, Stupid Love** •599

I hate love scenes in which the woman's naked and the man's wearing a three-piece suit. I mean fair's fair.

Julia Roberts •600

With most fellas, if you say something like "my favourite season's Autumn," they go "Oh, my favourite season's Spring." And then they go ten minutes talking about why they like spring. And you're not talking about Spring. You're talking about Autumn. So what you do? Talk about what they want to talk about, or you don't talk at all. Or you wind up talking to yourself.

Pauline Collins as Shirley Valentine •601

Gerry, I'm a woman! We don't say what we want!
But we reserve the right to get pissed off if we don't get it.
That's what makes us so fascinating! And not a little bit scary.

Jeanne Tripplehorn as Lydia in **Sliding Doors** •602

150

Well, if you're waitin' for a woman to make up her mind, you may have a long wait.

Clint Eastwood as The Preacher in **Pale Rider** •603

Harry: No man can be friends with a woman that he finds attractive. He always wants to have sex with her. Sally: So you're saying that a man can be friends with a woman he finds unattractive? Harry: No. You pretty much want to nail them too.

Billy Crystal and Meg Ryan in **When Harry Met Sally** •604

Alice: Because I'm a beautiful woman the only reason any man wants to talk to me is because he wants to fuck me? Is that what you're saying? Bill: Well, I don't think it's quite that black and white — but I think we both know what men are like.

Nicole Kidman and Tom Cruise in **Eyes Wide Shut** •605

Men are rats, listen to me, they're fleas on rats, worse than that, they're amoebas on fleas on rats. I mean, they're too low for even the dogs to bite. The only man a girl can depend on is her daddy. *Didi Conn as Frenchy in* **Grease** •606

151

They let 'em smoke and drive. They even put 'em in pants.
And what do you get? A democrat for President.

Prize dialogue from **Faster, Pussycat! Kill! Kill!** •607

Ben: Do you want to do it doggie style?
Allison: You're not going to fuck me like a dog.
Ben: It's doggie style. It's just the style. We don't
have to go outside or anything.

Seth Rogen and Katherine Heigl in **Knocked Up** •608

It is possible that blondes also prefer gentlemen.

Mamie Van Doren •609

My street slang is an increasingly valid form of
expression. Most of the feminine pronouns do have
mocking, but not necessarily misogynistic, undertones.

Donald Adesoun Faison as Murray, in **Clueless** •610

The man is the head but the woman is the neck.
She can turn the head any way she wants.

Lainie Kazan as Maria in **My Big Fat Greek Wedding** •611

Do you see a wedding ring on my finger? Does this place look like I'm fucking married? The toilet seat's up, man!

Jeff Bridges as The Dude in **The Big Lebowski** •612

Receptionist: How do you write women so well?
Melvin: I think of a man, and I take away reason and accountability.

Julie Benz and Jack Nicholson in **As Good As It Gets** •613

Never underestimate a man's ability to underestimate a woman. *Kathleen Turner as V.I.Warshawski* •614

Wendy?… Darling. Light of my life. I'm not gonna hurt ya. You didn't let me finish my sentence. I said: 'I'm not gonna hurt ya.' I'm just gonna bash your brains in. I'm gonna bash 'em right the fuck in!

Wendy Torrance (Sheely Duvall) realises her relationship with her husband is not what it was… **The Shining** •615

God gave men brains larger than dogs' so they wouldn't hump women's legs at cocktail parties.

Angelina Jolie as Kate Libby in **Hackers** •616

Oh, men. I never yet met one of them who didn't have the instincts of a heel. *Eve Arden as Ida in* **Mildred Pierce** •617

Rebecca: I thought sentiment made you uncomfortable.
Peter: I can handle it as long as it's disguised as sex.
Margaret Colin and Tom Selleck in **Three Men and A Baby** •618

You know what Joe wants. It's what all the Joes want.
Laurence Harvey as Joe Lampton in **Room At The Top** •619

Men are those creatures with two legs and eight hands.
Jayne Mansfield •620

All I'm trying to say is that there's lots of things that a man can do and in society's eyes it's all hunky dory. A woman does the same thing; the same thing, mind you – and she's an outcast. *Katharine Hepburn as Amanda in* **Adam's Rib** •621

I'm old fashioned. I like two sexes.
Spencer Tracy as Adam Bonner in **Adam's Rib** •622

If a man does something silly, people say, "isn't he silly?" If a woman does something silly, people say, "aren't women silly?"

Doris Day •623

Funny business, a woman's career. The things that you drop on your way up the ladder so you can move faster, you forget you'll need them again when you get back to being a woman. There's one career all females have in common – whether we like it or not – being a woman. *Bette Davis as Margo in* **All About Eve** •624

I was always in the kitchen. I felt as though I'd been born in a kitchen and lived there all my life except for the few hours it took me to get married.

Joan Crawford in **Mildred Pierce** •625

Lawrence: I wish you wouldn't call yourself a housewife. You're so much more than that.
Kate: So is every other housewife.

David Niven and Doris Day in **Please Don't Eat The Daisies** •626

The practice of putting women on pedestals began to die out when it was discovered that they could give orders better from that position. *Betty Grable* •627

No one should have to dance backward all their lives – this women's movement is as important as anti-slavery was in the 19th century.

Jane Fonda •628

Marion: You're not the same man I knew ten years ago.
Indiana Jones: It's not the years, honey, it's the mileage.
Karen Allen and Harrison Ford in **Raiders of the Lost Ark** •629

Vallo: Why did you bolt your cabin door last night?
Consuela: If you knew it was bolted you must have tried it. If you tried it, you know why it was bolted.
Burt Lancaster and Eva Bartok in **The Crimson Pirate** •630

Vince Stone: Hey, that's a nice perfume.
Debby Marsh: Something new. Attracts mosquitoes and repels men.
Lee Marvin and Gloria Grahame in **Big Heat** •631

Terry: What makes life so difficult?
Nickie: People?
Deborah Kerr and Cary Grant in **An Affair To Remember** •632

Felix: It's funny — I haven't thought of women in weeks.
Oscar: I fail to see the humor. *Lemmon & Matthau in* **The Odd Couple** •633

Janet: What have you done to Brad?
Frank N Furter: Nothing. Why, do you think I should?
Susan Sarandon and Tim Curry in **The Rocky Horror Picture Show** •634

Sidney: I have never hidden behind closet doors, but I am discreet.
Diana: Discreet? You did everything but lick his artichoke.
*Michael Caine and Maggie Smith in **California Suite** •635*

Helen: Do you really edit sex manuals?
George: I really, really do, but I have a confession to make.
I'm much better at books on gardening.
*Jill Clayburgh and Gene Wilder in **Silver Streak** •636*

Rod: I had a hard-on this morning and it had your
name written on it.
Tina: My name's four letters – there ain't enough
room on your john to fit it.
*Jsu Garcia And Amanda Wyss in **A Nightmare On Elm Street** •637*

Teddy: Did your mother ever wash your mouth out with soap and water?
Sam: Yeah, but it didn't do any fucking good.
*Glenn Close and Robert Loggia in **Jagged Edge** •638*

Cyphre: Are you an atheist?
Angel: Yeah, I'm from Brooklyn.
*Robert De Niro and Mickey Rourke in **Angel Heart** •639*

Jack: You look good.
Susie: You look like shit.
Jack: No, I mean it. You look good.
Susie: I mean it, too. You look like shit.
*Jeff Bridges and Michelle Pfeiffer in **The Fabulous Baker Boys** •640*

Vicki: Well, face it. You're not exactly normal, are you?
Batman: This isn't exactly a normal world, is it?
Kim Basinger and Michael Keaton in **Batman** •641

John Connor: You gotta listen to the way people talk. You don't say "affirmative," or some shit like that. You say "no problemo." And if someone comes on to you with an attitude you say "eat me." And if you want to shine them it's "hasta la vista, baby."
Terminator: Hasta la vista, baby!
John: Yeah! Or "later dickwad." And if someone gets upset you say, "chill out"! Or you can do combinations.
Terminator: Chill out, dickwad.
John: Great! See, you're getting it!
Terminator: No problemo.
Edward Furlong gives Arnie a language lesson in
Terminator2: Judgment Day •642

Harriet: What do you look for in a woman you date?
Charly: This is where everyone always says sense of humour – but I'd have to go for breast size.
Nancy Travis and Mike Myers in
So I Married An Axe Murderer •643

Bernadette: I'll join this conversation on the proviso that we stop bitching about people, talking about wigs, dresses, bust size, penises, drugs, night clubs and bloody Abba.
Tick: Doesn't give us much to talk about then, does it?
Terence Stamp and Hugo Weaving in **The Adventures of Priscilla, Queen of The Desert** •644

Marcus: Hey, man, where's your cup-holder?
Mike: I don't have one.
Marcus: What the fu — wha' you mean you don't have one? Eighty thousand dollars for this car and you ain't got no damn cup holder?
Martin Lawrence and Will Smith in **Bad Boys** •645

Dennis: Excuse me, can I just stop you there?
Whit: What .....?
Dennis: I don't have anything to say. I just wanted to stop you there.
Simon Pegg and Hank Azaria in **Run, Fat Boy, Run** •646

Ray Bones: Let me explain something to you. Momo is dead. Which means that everything he had now belongs to Jimmy Cap, including you. Which also means, that when I speak, I speak for Jimmy. e.g., from now on, you start showing me the proper fucking respect.
Chilli Palmer: "e.g." means "for example". What I think you want to say is "i.e.".
Dennis Farina and John Travolta discuss grammar in **Get Shorty** •647

Max: My teacher tells me beauty is on the inside.
Fletcher: That's just something ugly people say.
Justin Cooper and Jim Carrey in **Liar Liar** •648

Greyo: Dylan Thomas called Swansea "an ugly, lovely town".
Terry: I'd call it … a Pretty Shitty City.
Greyo: Dylan Thomas didn't do as much fucking cocaine as you, did he?

Dorien Thomas and Dougray Scott in **Twin Town** •649

Nick The Greek: Seems expensive.
Tom: Seems? Well, this seems to be a complete waste of my time. That, my friend, is 900 nicker in any store you're lucky enough to find one in. And you're haggling over 200 pound? What school of finance did you come from Nick? "It's a deal, it's a steal, it's the Sale of the fucking Century!" In fact, fuck it Nick, I think I'll keep it!

Stephen Marcus and Jason Flemyng in **Lock Stock and Two Smoking Barrels** •650

Carolyn: Are you trying to look unattractive?
Jane: Yes.
Carolyn: Well, congratulations, you've succeeded admirably.

Annette Bening and Thora Birch as mother and daughter in **American Beauty** •651

Sebastian: How is your gold-digging whore of a mother enjoying Bali?
Kathryn: She suspects your impotent, alcoholic father is diddling the maid.

Ryan Phillippe and Sarah Michelle Gellar as loving half-siblings in **Cruel Intentions** •652

Snowbell: Didn't your mother warn you that you shouldn't go out into Central Park at night?
Smokey: My mother was the reason you shouldn't go out into Central Park at night.

Nathan Lane and Chazz Palminteri as the voices of the cats, Snowbell and Smokey, in **Stuart Little** •653

Tommy: Do you accept Jesus Christ as your personal Lord and Saviour?
Hedwig: No, but I love his work.
Michael Pitt and John Cameron Mitchell in **Hedwig and the Angry Inch** •654

Christine: You will end up childless and alone.
Will: Well, fingers crossed, yeah.
Sharon Small and Hugh Grant in **About A Boy** •655

Phil Wenneck: The Best Little Chapel… do you know where that is?
Dr. Valsh: I do, it's at the corner of get a map and fuck off. I'm a doctor, not a tour guide.
Bradley Cooper as Phil and Matt Walsh as the Doctor in **The Hangover** •656

Annie: None of us have been here before, love. I mean, for God's sake, my John didn't see me naked until the spring of 1975.
Chris: What happened in the spring of '75?
Annie: There was a lizard in the shower block at Abergele.
Julie Walters and Helen Mirren in **Calendar Girls** •657

April: Can I ask you a personal question?
Walt: Nine inches.
Eva Mendes and Greg Kinnear in **Stuck On You** •658

Young Ed: I just saw the woman I'm going to marry. I know it. But I lost her.
Amos: Oh, tough break. Well, most men have to get married before they lose their wives.
Ewan McGregor and Danny DeVito in **Big Fish** •659

Howard Hughes: Will you marry me?
Ava Gardner: You're too crazy for me.
Leo DiCaprio and Kate Beckinsale in **The Aviator** •660

Mason: Are you sure you're ready for this?
Stanley: I'll do my best.
Mason: Your best? Losers always whine about their best. Winners go home and fuck the prom queen.
Sean Connery's Mason "motivates" Nic Cage's Stanly in **The Rock** •661

Sam: I haven't even lied in, like, the past two days.
Andrew: Is that true?
Sam: No.
Natalie Portman and Zach Braff in **Garden State** •662

Spooner: You have got to be the dumbest smart person I have ever met.
Susan Calvin: And *you* have got to be the dumbest *dumb* person I have ever met.
Will Smith and Bridget Moynahan in **I, Robot** •663

The world's most famous dirty old man.

Joe Queenan on Woody Allen •664

I appreciate the chance to visit my mom on Mother's Day — it's like taking a refresher course in guilt.

Woody Allen •665

Life is divided up into the horrible and the miserable.

Woody as Alvy Singer in **Annie Hall** •666

Achilles only had his heel. I've got an Achilles body.

Woody as Lenny in **Mighty Aphrodite** •667

Don't knock masturbation. It's sex with someone I love.

Woody in **Annie Hall** •668

The last time I was inside a woman was when I visited the Statue of Liberty.

Woody in **Crimes and Misdemeanours** •669

Look at all these people, trying to stave off the inevitable decay of their bodies.

Woody as Mickey in **Hannah and Her Sisters,** *talking about joggers* •670

My deepest apology goes to the Trochman family in Detroit.
I… I never delivered a baby before in my life,
and I… I just thought that ice tongs was the way to do it.

Woody as Leonard Zelig •671

Mother: Pay more attention to your schoolwork
and less to the radio.
Little Joe: You always listen to the radio.
Mother: It's different. Our lives are ruined already.

Julie Kavner and Seth Green in **Radio Days** •672

I remember when I was a little boy, I went and stole a pornographic book that was printed in braille. I used to rub the dirty parts.

Woody in **Bananas** •673

Ray (to his wife): What would you say if I told you you were married to a brilliant man?
Frenchy: I'd say I was a bigamist.

Woody and Tracey Ullman in **Small Time Crooks** •674

I like the way you express yourself too, you know. It's pithy, yet degenerate.

Woody as Isaac to Diane Keaton as Mary in **Manhattan** •675

There's nothing wrong with you that a little Prozac and a polo mallet can't cure.

Woody as Larry in **Manhattan Murder Mystery** •676

Arlene and I have to get a divorce. She thinks I'm a pervert because I drank our water bed.

Woody in **Sleeper** •677

That's okay we can walk to the curb from here.

Woody comments on Diane Keaton's parking in **Annie Hall** •678

167

Nobody's gonna be wearing beige
to a bank robbery; it's in poor taste.

Woody as Virgil Starkwell to Janet Margolin in **Take The Money and Run** •679

Nancy: You're immature, Fielding.
Fielding: How am I immature?
Nancy: Well, emotionally, sexually and intellectually.
Fielding: Yeah, but what other ways?

Louise Lasser and Woody in **Bananas** •680

Drew Barrymore sings so badly, deaf people refuse to watch her lips move.

Woody Allen •681

I don't mean much to the *Rambo* crowd.

Woody Allen •682

In real life, Keaton believes in God. But she also believes that the radio works because there are tiny people inside it.

Woody on Diane Keaton •683

Congratulations! He's a great director. Just don't have babies by him.

Mia Farrow advises Jim Broadbent on working for Woody Allen •684

If my films don't make a profit, I know I'm doing something right.

Woody Allen refuses to play the Hollywood game•685

My husband and I fell in love at first sight. Maybe I should have taken a second look.

Mia Farrow in **Crimes and Misdemeanours** •686

Vantine: (forced to share a room with the unsavoury Guidon)
Oh, please you guys! This place is full of lizards and cockroaches.
Carson: One more won't hurt.
Jean Harlow and Clark Gable in **Red Dust** •687

As long as they've got sidewalks, you've got a job.
Joan Blondell as Nan in **Footlight Parade** •688

Ask that common little woman to the house with that noisy, vulgar man? He smells Oklahoma!
Billie Burke as Mrs Jordan in **Dinner At Eight** •689

I don't like crooks. And if I did like 'em, I wouldn't like crooks that are stool pigeons. And if I did like crooks that are stool pigeons, I still wouldn't like you.
Gertrude Short as Marion in **The Thin Man** •690

By the way, there's a name for you ladies, but it isn't used in high society outside of a kennel.
Joan Crawford as Crystal Allen in **The Women** •691

170

She's got those eyes that run up
and down men like a searchlight.

Dennie Moore as Olga on Joan Crawford as Crystal in **The Women** •692

The only real native of Kansas is the buffalo.
He's got a very hard head, a very uncertain
temper, and a very lonely future. Apart from that,
there's hardly any comparison between you.

Errol Flynn as Wade Hatton to Olivia De Havilland in **Dodge City** •693

Benjamin is nobody's friend. If Benjamin were
an ice cream flavour, he'd be pralines and dick.

Dana Carvey as Garth in **Wayne's World**•694

Gentlemen, will you all now leave
quietly, or shall I ask Miss Cutler to
pass among you with a baseball bat?

Monty Woolley as Sheridan Whiteside in **The Man Who Came To Dinner** •695

Nice speech, Eve, but I wouldn't worry too much about your heart. You can always put that award where your heart ought to be. *Bette Davis as Margo in* **All About Eve** •696

I'd hate to take a bite out of you – you're a cookie full of arsenic.

Burt Lancaster as J.J. Hunsecker in **The Sweet Smell of Success** •697

As an actor, no one could touch him. As a human being, no one wanted to touch him.

Walter Matthau as Willy Clark, on George Burns in **The Sunshine Boys** •698

Tom Roberts is so boring his brother is an only child.

P.J.Soles as Riff in **Rock'n'Roll High School** •699

Ugarte: You despise me, don't you?
Rick: If I gave you any thought, I probably would.
Humphrey Bogart gives Peter Lorre short shrift in **Casablanca** •700

Steff: I've been out with a lot of girls at this school.
I don't see what makes you so different.
Andie: I have some taste.

James Spader and Molly Ringwald in **Pretty In Pink** •701

If I had a nose like Florine, I wouldn't go
around saying Merry Christmas to anybody.

Jessica Tandy as Daisy in **Driving Miss Daisy** •702

Truvy: You know, I'd rather walk on my lips than to criticise
anybody, but Janice Van Meter, I bet you she's paid $500 for
that dress and don't even bother to wear a girdle.
Clairee: Looks like two pigs fighting under a blanket.

Dolly Parton and Olympia Dukakis in **Steel Magnolias** •703

Myra Langtry: I'm Roy's friend.
Lilly Dillon: Yes. I imagine you're
lots of people's friend.

Annette Bening and Anjelica Huston in **The Grifters** •704

Daniel: I feel like Gloria Swanson.
Frank: You look like her mother.

Robin Williams and Harvey Fierstein in **Mrs Doubtfire** •705

173

Nicole's having an affair with Chook. Muriel saw them fucking in the laundry on your wedding day. Stick your drink up your ass, Tania. I'd rather swallow razor blades than have a drink with you.

Rachel Griffiths as Rhonda, telling Sophie Lee how it is in **Muriel's Wedding** •706

Cher: I want to do something good for humanity.
Josh: Try sterilisation.

Alicia Silverstone and Paul Rudd in **Clueless** •707

What's the décor?
Early Mexican brothel?

Judi Dench as Armande in **Chocolat** •708

Your mother was a hamster and
your father smelled of elderberries!

Insulting French soldier in **Monty Python and The Holy Grail** •709

This isn't "have a gimp over for dinner night, is it?"

Jon Voight as Luke in **Coming Home** •710

Sir, these letters are unequivocal, e.g. "Hey, Hauk. Eat a
bag of shit. You suck." Now that's pretty much to the
point, sir, not much gray area in this one.

Robert Wuhl as Staff Sgt Dreiwitz in **Good Morning, Vietnam** •711

I'd almost forgotten what your eyes looked like.
They're still the same. Piss-holes in the snow.

Michael Caine as Jack Carter in **Get Carter** •712

I think people who talk in metaphors
ought to shampoo my crotch.

Jack Nicholson as Melvin Udall in **As Good As It Gets** •713

Howard's End? Sounds filthy, doesn't it?

Julie Walters as Rita in **Educating Rita** •714

175

Mitzi: I never heard trumpet play.
Bernadette: Play? He didn't play, dear. Trumpet didn't have a single musical bone in his body. No, Trumpet had an unusually large foreskin. So large that he could wrap the entire thing around a Monte Carlo biscuit.

Hugo Weaving and Terence Stamp in
Adventures of Priscilla, Queen of the Desert •715

There are two things I hate about you, Felicia. Your face. So shut both of them.

Hugo Weaving as Tick in **The Adventures of Priscilla, Queen of The Desert** •716

Oh man, shut your anorexic, malnutrition tapeworm-having, overdose-on-Dick-Gregory, Bohemian, diet-drinking ass up.

Wesley Snipes as Sidney Deane in **White Men Can't Jump** •717

One more push, I'm gonna smack his face so hard he'll have to stick his toothbrush up his arse to clean his teeth! *Terence Stamp as Bernadette in* **Adventures of Priscilla, Queen of the Desert** •718

To call you stupid would be an insult to stupid people. I've known sheep that could outwit you; I've worn dresses with higher IQs. But you think you're an intellectual, don't you, ape?

Jamie Lee Curtis as Wanda in **A Fish Called Wanda** •719

Mookie: Pino, fuck you, fuck your fuckin' pizza, and fuck Frank Sinatra.
Pino: Yeah? Well fuck you too, and fuck Michael Jackson.

Spike Lee and John Turturro discussing racial differences in **Do The Right Thing** •720

I hope all your children have very small dicks! And that includes the girls!

Jeff Goldblum as Dexter in **The Tall Guy** •721

Deputy Doofy: Mom said that when I wear this badge you're supposed to treat me like a man of the law.
Buffy: Yeah, and Mom also said for you to stop sticking your dick in the vacuum cleaner!

Dave Sheridan and Anna Faris in **Scary Movie** •722

Dante: Embolism in a pool. What an embarrassing way to die.
Randal: That's nothing compared to how my cousin Walter died.
Dante: How did he die?
Randal: He broke his neck.
Dante: That's not embarrassing.
Randal: He broke his neck trying to suck his own dick.

Brian O'Halloran and Jeff Anderson in **Clerks** •723

177

Man: Hey, vodka rocks, what do you say you and
me get nipple to nipple?
Large breasted girl: I can do that without you.

Banter from **Road House** •724

My brother wouldn't touch your titties with a ten foot
pole. He likes his women bad, Lenora, not cheap.

Rikki Lake as Pepper in **Cry-Baby** •725

You know your business, I know mine. Your business is being an asshole.

Al Pacino, as Ricky Roma, to Kevin Spacey in **Glengarry Glen Ross** •726

I apologise for the intelligence of my remarks, Sir Thomas,
I had forgotten that you were a Member of Parliament.

George Sanders as Sir Henry in **The Picture of Dorian Gray** •727

This stuff is beyond crap. It is what crap wants to be when it grows up.

Gregory Smith as Sport in **Harriet The Spy** •728

It wasn't what I did, but how I did it. It wasn't what I said but how I said it, and how I looked when I did and said it.

Mae West •729

It's not the men in my life but the life in my men.

Mae West in **I'm No Angel** •730

When I'm good, I'm very very good. But when I'm bad, I'm better.

Mae West in **I'm No Angel** •731

To err is human, but it feels divine.

Mae West •732

I've been getting by for years on what I didn't show the boys.

Mae West •733

179

I generally avoid temptation, unless I can't resist it.

Mae West as Flower Belle Lee in **My Little Chickadee** •734

I always did like a man in a uniform. And that one
fits you grand. Why don't you come up some time
and see me? I'm home every evening.

Mae West to Cary Grant; the oft misquoted lines from **She Done Him Wrong** •735

Every man I meet wants to protect
me. I can't figure out what from.

Mae West as Flower Belle Lee in **My Little Chickadee** •736

Between two evils, I always pick the
one I haven't tried before.

Mae West as Mavis in **Go West, Young Man** •737

When women go wrong, men go right after them.

Mae West in **She Done Him Wrong** •738

180

You gotta get up early in the morning to catch a fox and stay up late at night to get a mink.
Mae West •739

Hi, handsome, is that a ten-gallon hat or are you just enjoying the show.
Madeleine Kahn as Lili von Shtupp, a Mae West parody, in **Blazing Saddles** •740

I… found it a good policy to slip a few items into a script the censors would cut out. It gave them a sense of accomplishing their job, and they were less likely to cut out the things I really wanted to keep in. *Mae West* •741

I didn't invent sex, I just rediscovered it, uncovered it, and give it a couple of definitions that Mr Webster never thought of. *Mae West* •742

She was the kind of girl who climbed the ladder of success wrong by wrong.
Mae West on Jean Harlow •743

Someone has stolen the cork out of my lunch!

W.C. Fields, on the set of **My Little Chickadee,** *according to Mae West* •745

She drove me to drink. That's the
one thing I'm indebted to her for.

W. C. Fields, **Never Give a Sucker an Even Break** •746

Drown in a vat of liquor? Death, where is thy sting?

W.C. Fields as The Great Man in **Never Give A Sucker An Even Break** •747

Everything I like to do is either
illegal, immoral or fattening.

W.C. Fields in **Never Give A Sucker An Even Break** •748

They say that drinking interferes with your
sex life. I figure it's the other way around.

W.C. Fields •749

I make it a habit to keep a reasonable supply of medicinal stimulants on hand in case I encounter a venomous snake – which I also always keep on hand.

W.C. Fields •750

It's hard to tell where Hollywood ends and the DTs begin.

W.C. Fields •751

I feel as though the Russian army had been walking over my tongue in their stocking feet.

W.C. Fields as Sheriff Hoxley in **Six of A Kind** •752

I ought to write a book: *The Art of Arising The Morning After.*

W.C. Fields as Twillie in **My Little Chickadee** •753

I never smoked a cigarette until I was nine.

W.C. Fields as Egbert Souse •754

A thing worth having is worth cheating for.

W.C. Fields as Twillie in **My Little Chickadee** •755

Marry an outdoor woman. Then if you throw her
out in the yard for the night, she can still survive.

W.C. Fields •756

I am free of all prejudice.
I hate everybody equally.

W.C. Fields •757

Give him an evasive answer.
Tell him to go fuck himself.

W.C. Fields gives a message to a studio executive •758

Annual income twenty pounds, annual expenditure nineteen pounds; result – happiness. Annual income twenty pounds, annual expenditure twenty-one pounds; result – misery.

W.C. Fields as Micawber in **David Copperfield** •759

Though he looked like a brimming Toby jug, it was always clear that no mantelpiece would hold him.

Kenneth Tynan •760

How's it hangin', Death?

Keanu Reeves as Ted, fails to pay due deference to the Grim Reaper in **Bill & Ted's Bogus Journey** •761

History Teacher: Who was Joan of Arc? Ted: Noah's wife?

Keanu Reeves as Ted makes an (un)educated guess in **Bill & Ted's Excellent Adventure** •762

Ted: I'm in love, dude.
Bill: Come on, this is a history report not a babe report.
Ted: Bill, those are historical babes.
Bill: OK, you're the ladies man. How we gonna meet 'em?
Keanu Reeves and Alex Winter in **Bill & Ted's Excellent Adventure** •763

Stay here and do nothing. If you do nothing, nothing can go wrong.

Peter MacNicol as David Langley in **Bean** •764

It's a topsy-turvy world, Jane. And maybe the problems of two people don't amount to a hill of beans, but this is our hill, and these are our beans.
Leslie Nielsen as Frank Drebin in **Naked Gun** •765

Jane: Would you like a night-cap? Drebin: No, thank you. I don't wear them.

Priscilla Presley and Leslie Nielsen in **Naked Gun** •766

Khasi of Kalabar: May the great God Shivoo bring blessings on your house.
Sir Sidney Ruff-Diamond: And on yours.
Khasi: Any may his radiance light up your darkness.
Sidney: And up yours.
Kenneth Williams and Sid James in **Carry On Up The Khyber** •767

Matron: I'm a simple woman with simple tastes, and I want to be wooed!
Sir Bernard: Ooh, you can be as 'wude' as you like with me!
Hattie Jacques and Kenneth Williams in **Carry On Matron** •768

If you were thrilled by *The Towering Inferno*, if you were terrified by *Earthquake*, then you will be SCARED SHITLESS at the Samuel L. Bronkowitz production of *That's Armageddon!* **Kentucky Fried Movie** •769

That's exactly why we want to produce this play. To show the world the true Hitler, the Hitler you loved, the Hitler you knew, the Hitler with a song in his heart. *Zero Mostel as Max Bialystock in* **The Producers** •770

There was a time when I used to get lots of ideas…
I thought up the Seven Deadly Sins in one afternoon.
The only thing I've come up with recently is advertising.
Peter Cook as Spiggott in **Bedazzled** •771

It's not easy being the Barbara Streisand of Evil.
Liz Hurley as The Devil in **Bedazzled** •772

See, there's three kinds of people: dicks, pussies, and assholes. Pussies think everyone can get along, and dicks just want to fuck all the time without thinking it through. But then you got your assholes, Chuck. And all the assholes want us to shit all over everything! So, pussies may get mad at dicks once in a while, because pussies get fucked by dicks. But dicks also fuck assholes, Chuck. And if they didn't fuck the assholes, you know what you'd get? You'd get your dick and your pussy all covered in shit!

A guy in a bar dispenses key advice in
Team America : World Police •773

Black Knight: Had enough eh?
King Arthur: Look, you stupid bastard. You've got no arms left.
BK: Yes I have.
KA: Look!
BK: Just a flesh wound.

Graham Chapman and John Cleese in **Monty Python and the Holy Grail** •774

Satan: How come you always want to make love to me from behind? Is it because you want to pretend I'm somebody else?
Saddam Hussein: Satan, your ass is gigantic and red. Who am I going to pretend you are, Liza Minelli?

South Park: Bigger Longer Uncut *(voices of Trey Parker and Matt Stone)* •775

You put a greased, naked woman on all fours, with a dog collar around her neck, and a leash, and the man's arm extended out up to here, holding on to the leash and pushing a black glove in her face to sniff it. You don't find that offensive?

Fran Deschler as Bobbi, debating **Spinal Tap's** *new album cover* •776

Do me a favor. Just kick my ass, okay? Kick this ass for a man, that's all. Kick my ass. Enjoy. Come on. I'm not asking, I'm telling with this. Kick my ass.

Paul Shaffer as Artie Fufkin in **This Is Spinal Tap** •777

190

Man, I don't drop character 'til I done the DVD commentary.
Robert Downey jr as method actor Kirk Lazarus in **Tropic Thunder** •778

As long as people are still having premarital sex with many anonymous partners while at the same time experimenting with mind expanding drugs in a consequence free environment, I'll be sound as a pound! *Mike Myers as* **Austin Powers** •779

There's no reason to become alarmed, and we hope you'll enjoy the rest of your flight. By the way, is there anyone on board who knows how to fly a plane?
Julie Hagerty as Elaine in **Airplane!** •780

Have you ever seen a grown man naked, Joey? •781

…Joey, do you like films about gladiators? •782

…Joey, have you ever been in a Turkish prison? •783
Peter Graves as Captain Oveur, questions young passenger in **Airplane!**

Cancel the kitchen scraps for lepers and orphans. No more merciful beheadings. And call off Christmas.
Alan Rickman as the Sheriff of Nottingham in **Robin Hood, Prince of Thieves** •784

191

Phil Connors: Do you ever have déjà vu, Mrs Lancaster?
Mrs Lancaster: I don't know. I'll ask in the kitchen.
Bill Murray and Angela Paton in **Groundhog Day** •785

The weather out there today is hot and shitty with continued hot and shitty in the afternoon. Tomorrow a chance of continued crappy with a pissy weather front coming down from the north. Basically, it's hotter than a snake's ass in a wagon rut.
Robin Williams as Adria Cronauer in **Good Morning, Vietnam** •786

Well, yes mate. See, I'm dishonest. And a dishonest man you can always trust to be dishonest. Honestly. It's the honest ones you need to watch out for, because you never know when they're going to do something incredibly… stupid.
Johnny Depp as Captain Jack Sparrow in the first **Pirates of the Caribbean** *movie* •787

City Slickers was a hit all over the world except in France. I couldn't figure out why till they told me they changed the title to La Vie, L'amour et Les Vaches, which means Life, Love and Cows.
Billy Crystal •788

Ed Wood: I like to dress in women's clothing.
Georgie Weiss: You're a fruit?
Ed: No, not at all. I love women. Wearing their clothes makes me feel closer to them.
Georgie: You're not a fruit?
Ed: No, I'm all man. I even fought in W.W.2. Of course, I was wearing women's undergarments under my uniform.
Johnny Depp and Mike Starr in **Ed Wood** •789

192

Dr Forrest: Don't go near my daughter again. Don't try to see her. Don't write her and don't phone her.
Rigby: Can I use her underwear to make soup?
George Gaynes and Steve Martin in **Dead Men Don't Wear Plaid** •790

Frankenstein: I'm a brilliant surgeon, perhaps I can help you with that hump?
Igor: What hump? *Gene Wilder and Marty Feldman in* **Young Frankenstein** •791

Freb: You ever feel bad about any of this?
Donny: Hell, no. I'm Robin Hood, man.
I rob from the rich and give to the needy.
Freb: You mean the poor?
Donny: No, like I said, the needy. 'Cause brother, we need this car.
James Duval and Chi McBride in **Gone In Sixty Seconds** •792

I get goose pimples. Even my goose pimples get goose pimples.
Bob Hope as Wally in **The Cat and The Canary** •793

We're no longer called Sonic Death Monkey. We're on the verge of becoming Kathleen Turner Overdrive, but just for tonight, we are Barry Jive and his Uptown Five.
Jack Black as Barry in **High Fidelity** •794

Dana Barrett: Do you want this body?
Venkman: Is this a trick question?
Signourney Weaver and Bill Murray in **Ghostbusters** •795

Is that hair gel?
Cameron Diaz in **There's Something About Mary.**
It wasn't. •796

NO DINOSAURS WERE HARMED IN THE MAKING OF THIS MOTION PICTURE

The Flintstones •797

The only surefire way to test out a new gag was to try it on Zeppo. If he liked it, we threw it out. *Groucho Marx* •798

An amateur thinks it's funny if you dress a man up as an old lady, sit him in a wheelchair, and shove the wheelchair down a slope towards an approaching car. For a pro, it's got to be a real old lady. *Groucho* •799

Flo: I've never been so insulted in my life!
Hackenbush: Well, it's early yet.

Esther Muir and Groucho Marx in **A Day at the Races** •800

Bob: General Smith reports a gas attack.
He wants to know what to do.
Firefly: Tell him to take a teaspoonful of bicarbonate of soda and a half a glass of water.

Zeppo and Groucho in **Duck Soup** •801

I'll bet your father spent the first year
of your life throwing rocks at the stork.

Groucho as J. Cheever Loophole in **At The Circus** •802

I married your mother because I wanted children.
Imagine my disappointment when you arrived.

Groucho to Zeppo in **Horse Feathers** •803

Barovelli: There's a man outside with a big black moustache.
Wagstaff: Tell him I've got one.

Chico and Groucho in **Horse Feathers** •804

Barovelli, you've got the brain of a four-
year-old boy, and I'll bet he was glad to get
rid of it. *Groucho as Professor Wagstaff in* **Horse Feathers** •805

Gentlemen, Chicolini here may talk like an idiot, and look like
an idiot, but don't let that fool you: he really is an idiot.

Groucho as Rufus T. Firefly in **Duck Soup** •806

196

I'm in a hurry! To the House of Representatives!
Ride like fury! If you run out of gas, get ethyl.
If Ethel runs out, get Mabel! Now step on it!
Groucho as Rufus T. Firefly in **Duck Soup** •807

One morning I shot an elephant in my pajamas.
How he got into my pajamas I'll never know.
Groucho as Captain Spalding in **Animal Crackers** •808

Otis: If any of the parties participating in this contract is shown not
to be in their mind, the entire agreement is automatically nullified.
That's in every contract. That's what they call the sanity clause.
Fiorello: You can't fool me. There ain't no Sanity Clause!
Groucho and Chico in **A Night At The Opera** •809

You can leave in a taxi.
If you can't leave in a taxi,
you can leave in a huff.
If that's too soon, you can
leave in a minute and a huff.
Groucho as Firefly in **Duck Soup** •810

197

Mister you no understand. Look, he's a spy and I'm a spy, he work-a for me. I want him to find out-a something, but he no find out what I wanna find out. Now how am I gonna find out what I wanna find out if he no find out what I gotta find out? *Chico as Chicolini in* **Duck Soup** •811

Mrs Teasdale: My husband is dead.
Firefly: I'll bet he's just using that as an excuse.
Mrs Teasdale: I was with him to the end.
Firefly: No wonder he passed away.
Mrs Teasdale: I held him in my arms and kissed him.
Firefly: So it was murder!
Margaret Dumont and Groucho in **Duck Soup** •812

Remember, you're fighting for this woman's honour, which is probably more than she ever did. *Groucho as Firefly in* **Duck Soup** •813

Your eyes! They shine like the pants of blue serge suit. *Groucho as Hammer in* **The Cocoanuts** •814

I've respected your husband for
many years. What's good enough
for him is good enough for me.
Groucho in **Monkey Business** •815

Lulubelle, it's you! I didn't recognise you standing up.
Groucho as S. Quentin Quale in **Go West** •816

Beatrice: I'm Beatrice Ryner.
I stop at the hotel.
Kornblow: My name's Ronald Kornblow.
I stop at nothing.
Lisette Verea and Groucho in **A Night In Casablanca** •817

Emily, I have a little confession to make.
I really am a horse doctor. But marry me,
and I'll never look at any other horse.
Groucho as Hackenbush in **A Day at the Races** •818

Hackenbush: You know, I proposed to your mother once.

Judy: That's my father!

Hackenbush: No wonder he turned me down.

Groucho and Maureen O'Sullivan in
A Day At The Races •819

I could dance with you 'til the cows come home. On second thoughts, I'd rather dance with the cows 'til you came home.

Groucho as Firefly in **Duck Soup** •820

To me, being a gangster was better than being President of the United States.

Ray Liotta as Henry Hill in **Goodfellas** •872

Come out and take it, you dirty yellow-bellied rat, or I'll give it to you through the door.

James Cagney as Matt Nolan in **Taxi Driver**, *1931* •873

Your hands ain't so clean. You killed and liked it. You didn't get them medals by holding hands with them Germans. *James Cagney as Tom Powers in* **Public Enemy** •874

You been reading a lot of stuff about "crime don't pay". Don't be a sucker. That's for yaps and small timers on shoestrings. Not for people like us. You belong in the big shot class. Both of us do. *James Cagney as Rocky Sullivan in* **Angels with Dirty Faces** •875

Hally: I don't trust you.
Bartlett: Looks like you need a little watchin' yourself.
Hally: Sounds like the basis of a good partnership.

Bogart and Cagney in **The Roaring Twenties** •876

202

I'm forty-seven. Forty-seven years old. You know how I stayed alive this long?
Fear. Fearsome acts. A man steals from me, I cut off his hand. If
he lies to me, I cut out his tongue. If he stands up against me, I cut off his
head, stick it on a pike and lift it up for all to see. A spectacle of fearsome acts.
That's what maintains the order of things. Fear.
Daniel Day-Lewis as Bill The Butcher in **Gangs of New York** •877

You think ambushing me in some nightclub's gonna stop
what makes people take drugs? This country spends $100 billion
a year on getting high, and it's not because of me. All that time
I was wasting in jail, it just got worse. I'm not your problem. I'm
just a businessman. *Christopher Walken as Frank in* **King of New York** •878

Running a casino is like robbing a bank
with no cops around. For guys like me,
Las Vegas washes away your sins. It's
like a morality car wash. *Robert DeNiro as Ace*
Rothstein in **Casino** •879

It's all business. That's what you fail to grasp. And in business, you must
have something to trade. And you, Mr. Sullivan, have nothing to trade.
Dylan Baker as Rance in **Road To Perdition** •880

I don't feel that I have to wipe everybody out, Tom. Just my enemies, that's all.

Al Pacino as Michael Corleone in **The Godfather II** •881

If you point a gun at someone, you'd better make sure you shoot him, and if you shoot him you'd better make sure he's dead, because if he isn't then he's gonna get up and try to kill you.

John Getz as Ray in **Blood Simple** •882

If you walk through this door now, you're walking into a world of trouble, and there's no turning back, you understand?

Sean Connery as Malone in **The Untouchables** •883

I'll tell you right out; I'm a man who likes talking to a man who likes to talk.

Sydney Greenstreet as Kasper Gutman in **The Maltese Falcon** •884

Thousands of guys got guns, but there's only one Johnny Rocco.

Edward G Robinson as Rocco in **Key Largo** •885

This here's Miss Bonnie Parker. I'm Clyde Barrow.
We rob banks. *Warren Beatty in* **Bonnie and Clyde** •886

We want to hurt no one. We're here for the bank's money, not your
money. Your money is insured by the federal government, you're
not gonna lose a dime. Think of your families, don't risk your life.
Don't try and be a hero. *Robert De Niro as Neil McCauley*
in **Heat** •887

What the cops never figured out, and what I know now,
was that these men would never break, never
lie down, never bend over for anybody. Anybody.
Kevin Spacey as Verbal Kint in **The Usual Suspects** •888

Sarno: So, you the brains of this outfit, or is he?
Longbaugh: Tell you the truth, I don't think this
is a brains kind of operation.
James Caan and Benicio del Toro in **The Way of The Gun** •889

I worked for the people who worked for the people.

Burt Lancaster as Lou in **Atlantic City** •890

Rick: I came to Casablanca for the waters.
Renault: What waters? We're in the desert?
Rick: I was misinformed.
Bogart and Claude Rains in **Casablanca** •891

Ilsa: That was the day the Germans marched into Paris.
Rick: I remember every detail. The Germans wore grey. You wore blue.
Ingrid Bergman as Ilsa Lund and Bogart as Rick Blaine in **Casablanca** •892

I stick my neck out for nobody.
I'm the only cause I'm interested in.
Bogart in **Casablanca** •893

If she can stand it,
I can. Play it!

Bogart in **Casablanca**. •894

Was that gun fire, or is it my heart pounding?
Ingrid Bergman as Ilsa Lund in **Casablanca** •895

Rick: If that plane leaves the ground and you're not with him, you'll regret it – maybe not today, maybe not tomorrow, but soon, and for the rest of your life.
Ilsa: But what about us?
Rick: We'll always have Paris.

Bogart and Bergman in **Casablanca** •896

I'm hard to get, Steve. All you have to do is ask me.
Ingrid Bergman as Slim in **To Have and Have Not** •897

You know, Steve, you're not very hard to figure out at times. Sometimes I know exactly what you're going to say. The other times, you're just a stinker.
Lauren Bacall to Bogart in **To Have and Have Not** •898

Bogart fell in love with the character Bacall played in *To Have and Have Not*, so she had to keep playing it for the rest of his life. *Howard Hawks* •899

Humphrey Bogart always told me movies were like a slot machine. If you played long enough, you'd eventually hit the jackpot, which he did with *Maltese Falcon. Geraldine Fitzgerald* •900

When you're slapped, you'll take it and like it.

Bogart in **The Maltese Falcon** •901

My, my. Such a lot of guns around town and so few brains.

Bogart in **The Big Sleep** •902

I don't mind if you don't like my manners. I don't like them myself. They're pretty bad. I grieve over them long winter evenings.

Bogart as Marlowe in **The Big Sleep** •903

I liked that. I'd like more.

Lauren Bacall as Vivian in **The Big Sleep** •904

Marlowe: Speaking of horses… you've got a touch of class, but I don't know how far you can go.
Vivian: A lot depends on who's in the saddle.

Bogart and Bacall in **The Big Sleep** •905

Marlowe: What's wrong with you?
Vivian: Nothing you can't fix.

Bogart and Bacall in **The Big Sleep** •906

You don't like it, do you Rocco? The storm? Show it your gun, why don't you? If it doesn't stop, shoot it. *Bogart as Frank McLeod, taunting Edward G Robinson in* **Key Largo** •907

Do you look down on all women?
Or just the ones you know?

Gloria Grahame to Bogart in **In A Lonely Place** •908

There are four ways of doing things on board my ship. The right way, the wrong way, the navy way, and my way.
Bogart as Captain Queeg in **The Caine Mutiny** •909

A man alone, he gets to living like a hog.

Bogart as Allnutt in **The African Queen** •910

Bogart's a hell of a nice guy till 11:30 p.m. After that he thinks he's Bogart. *Dave Chasen* •911

How can a man so ugly be handsome?

Marta Torne as Violette, talking about Bogart in **Sirocco** •912

Come and have a go if you think you're hard enough.

Darren Morfitt as Spoon in **Dog Soldiers** •913

You tell him, you tell him I'm coming.
Tell him I'm fucking coming!

Terence Stamp as Wilson in **The Limey** •914

The son of a bitch is here. I saw him.
I'm gonna get him. *Gene Hackman as Popeye Doyle*
in **The French Connection** •915

In my situation, days are like women; each one's
so damn precious, but they all end up leaving you.
Darwin Joston as Napoleon Wilson in **Assault On Precinct 13** •916

I need your clothes, your boots and your motorcycle.
Arnie as The Terminator in **T2** •917

Old Baloo's going to learn you to fight like a bear!
Phil Harris as the voice of Baloo in **The Jungle Book** •918

I don't believe I ever killed a man that didn't deserve it. *John Wayne as Books in* **The Shootist** •919

I wanna shoot you so bad, my dick's hard!
Ice-T as Scotty in **New Jack City** •920

I want you on the next transport off this rock or I'm gonna shoot you where it don't grow back.
Tommy Lee Jones as Agent K in **Men In Black** •921

I'll hit you so hard, I'll kill your whole family.
Timothy Daly as Billy in **Diner** •922

I'll shove that bat up your ass and turn you into a popsicle. *James Remar as Angel in* **The Warriors** •923

You're a big man, but you're out of shape. With me it's a full-time job. Now behave yourself. *Michael Caine as Jack Carter in* **Get Carter** •924

I'm here to keep you alive, not help you shop.
Kevin Costner as Frank Farmer in **The Bodyguard** •925

> Mickey: I realised my true calling in life.
> Gale: What's that?
> Mickey: I'm a natural born killer.
> *Woody Harrelson and Robert Downey jnr in* **Natural Born Killers** •926

Helen: Have you ever killed anyone?
Harry: Yeah, but they were all bad.
Jamie Lee Curtis and Arnie in **True Lies** •927

Behold my Lord Ulrich! The rock! The hard place! Like a wind from Gelderland he sweeps by, blown far from his homeland in search of glory and honor. We walk in the garden of his turbulence.
Paul Bethany as Chaucer introduces Heath ledger at the jousts in **A Knight's Tale** •928

> My name is Maximus Decimus Meridius, Commander of the Armies of the North, General of the Felix Legions, loyal servant to the true emperor, Marcus Aurelius. Father to a murdered son, husband to a murdered wife. And I will have my vengeance, in this life or the next *Russell Crowe in* **Gladiator** •929

When you marooned me on that god forsaken spit
of land, you forgot one very important thing, mate:
I'm Captain Jack Sparrow.
Johnny Depp in **Pirates of the Caribbean** •930

I swear to God, if I even feel somebody behind me, there is no
measure to how fast and how hard I will bring this fight to your
doorstep. I'm on my own side now. *Matt Damon as Jason Bourne
in* **The Bourne Identity** •931

I'm not giving up, I'm just saying, "I'll never make it".
Giving up is when you can still make it, but you give up.
Jack Lemmon as George Kellerman in **The Out-of-Towners** •932

That's what makes us tough. Rich fellas come up and
they die and their kids ain't no good and they die out.
But we keep a' comin'. *Jane Darwell as Ma Joad in*
The Grapes of Wrath •933

I could've been a contender. I could've had
class and been somebody. Real class. Instead
of a bum, let's face it, which is what I am.
Marlon Brando as Terry Malloy in **On The Waterfront** •934

All you have to do is follow three simple rules. One, never underestimate your opponent. Expect the unexpected. Two, take it outside. Never start anything inside the bar unless it's absolutely necessary. And three, be nice.

Patrick Swayze defines the rules of bouncing as Dalton in **Road House** •935

You'll get a shitload of fish. I've gone out before and motored back with so much stock little boys like you had to pack it on the pier. I always find the fish, always! And I will this time. So don't fuck with me!

George Clooney as Captain Billy Tyne in **A Perfect Storm** •936

I once fought two days with an arrow through my testicle.

Liam Neeson as Godfrey of Ibelin in **Kingdom of Heaven** •937

If his unpleasant wounding has in some way enlightened the rest of you as to the grim finish beneath the glossy veneer of criminal life, then his injuries carry with it an inherent nobility, and a supreme glory. We should all be so fortunate. You say poor Toby? I say poor us. *Vinnie Jones as Sphinx, speaking for the first time in the last reel of* **Gone In Sixty Seconds** •938

What makes a two-bit heel like you think
a heater would give him an edge over me?
Preston Foster as Tim in **Kansas City Confidential** •939

An immaculate murder. We've killed for the
sake of danger and for the sake of killing.
John Dall as Brandon in **Rope** •940

The next person that says Merry Christmas to me, I'll kill them.
Myrna Loy as Nora in **The Thin Man** •941

I met a lot of hard-boiled eggs in my life, but you – you're 20 minutes.
Jan Sterling as Lorraine to Kirk Douglas in **Ace In The Hole** •942

Max: You'll live with the stink of the streets all your life.
Noodles: I like the stink of the streets. It cleans out my
lungs. And it gives me a hard-on.
James Woods and Robert De Niro in **Once Upon A Time in America** •943

I'm gonna keep the coke and the fries but I'm gonna send this
burger back. And if you put any mayonnaise on it, I'm gonna come
over to your house, I'll chop your legs off, set fire to your house,
and watch as you drag your bloody stumps out the door.
Bruce Willis as Jimmy The Tulip in **The Whole Nine Yards** •944

216

If you hold back anything, I'll kill ya. If you bend the truth or I think your bending the truth, I'll kill ya. If you forget anything, I'll kill ya. In fact, you're gonna have to work very hard to stay alive, Nick. Now do you understand everything I've said? Because if you don't, I'll kill ya. Vas Blackwood as Rory Breaker in **Lock, Stock and Two Smoking Barrels** •945

Also, I think knives are a good idea. Big, fuck-off shiny ones. Ones that look like they could skin a crocodile. Knives are good, because they don't make any noise, and the less noise they make, the more likely we are to use them. Shit 'em right up. Makes it look like we're serious. Guns for show, knives for a pro.
Dexter Fletcher as Soap in **Lock Stock and Two Smoking Barrels** •946

It's been emotional.
Vinnie Jones as Big Chris in **Lock, Stock and Two Smoking Barrels** •947

217

What is drama, after all, but
life with the dull bits cut out? •948

For me the cinema is not a
slice of life but a piece of cake.. •949

The length of the film should be directly related
to the endurance of the human bladder. •950

A good film is when the price of the dinner, the
theatre admission and the babysitter were worth it. •951

In film, murders are always very clean.
I show how difficult it is and what a
messy thing it is to kill a man.

(attrib) •952

I aim to provide the public with beneficial shocks. •953

Alfred Hitchcock, in his own words.

Actors are cattle. Disney probably has the right idea. He draws them and if he doesn't like them he tears them up. •954

My advice to young actors? Stay out of jail. •955

I always say that the most difficult things to photograph are dogs, babies, motor boats, Charles Laughton (God rest his soul), and method actors. •956

Life typecasts us. Look at me. Do you think I would've chosen to look like this? I would prefer to have played the leading man in life. I would have been Cary Grant. •957

If I made *Cinderella* people would be looking for the body in the coach. •958

Alfred Hitchcock, in his own words.

Alfred Hitchcock's interested in making your mind, rather than your flesh, creep. *Laura Baum* •959

Hitchcock filmed murder scenes as if they were love scenes and love scenes as if they were murder scenes. *François Truffaut* •960

Kim Novak: Mr Hitchcock, what is my character feeling in relation to her surroundings? Hitchcock: It's only a movie, for God's sake. *As related by James Stewart* •961

Foreigners somehow expect the squares of London to be fog-weaved, full of hansom cabs and littered with ripped whores. *John Boxer as Sir George in* **Frenzy** •962

Right now, I'd welcome trouble.
James Stewart as Jeff in **Rear Window** •963

220

I say that you cannot administer a wicked law impartially. You can only destroy. You can only punish. And I warn you that a wicked law, like cholera, destroys everyone it touches; its upholders, as well as its defiers. *Spencer Tracy as Henry Drummond, in* **Inherit The Wind** •964

Now gentlemen, in this country our courts are the great levelers, and in our courts all men are created equal. I'm no idealist to believe firmly in the integrity of our courts and of our jury system. That's no ideal to me. That is a living, working reality. *Gregory Peck as Atticus Finch in* **To Kill A Mockingbird** •965

There were eleven votes for guilty. It's not easy to raise my hand and send a boy off to die without talking about it first.

Henry Fonda as Davis in **Twelve Angry Men** •966

Mickey: Do you know who the attorney is for the defense? Ed Concannon!
Frank: He's a good man …
Mickey: He's a good man? He's the Prince of fucking Darkness! He'll have people testifying they saw her waterskiing up in Marblehead last summer. Frank, don't fuck with this case!

Jack Warden and Paul Newman in **The Verdict** •967

Your Honour, with all due respect, if you're going to try my case for me, I wish you wouldn't lose it.

Paul Newman as Frank Galvin in **The Verdict** •968

Today, you are the law. You are the law. Not some book. Not the lawyers. Not a marble statue, or the trappings of the court. See, those are just symbols of our desire to be just. They are, in fact, a prayer. A fervent and a frightened prayer.

Paul Newman as Frank Galvin in **The Verdict** •969

The prosecution would like to separate the motive from the act. Well, that's like trying to take the core from an apple without breaking the skin.

James Stewart as Paul Biegler in **Anatomy of a Murder** •970

I object, your honour. This trial is a travesty. It's a travesty of a mockery of a sham of a mockery of a travesty of two mockeries of a sham.

Woody Allen as Fielding Mellish in **Bananas** •971

Major Tetley: Other men with families have had to die for this sort of thing. It's too bad, but it's justice.
Donald Martin: Justice? What do you care about justice? You don't even care whether you've got the right men or not. All you know is you've lost something and somebody's got to be punished. *Frank Conroy and Dana Andrews*
in **The Ox-Bow Incident** •972

Justice and law are distant cousins. They're not on speaking terms at all.

Marlon Brando as Ian McKenzie in **A Dry White Season** •973

If you want justice, go to a whorehouse. If you want to be fucked, go to court.

Richard Gere as Martin Vail in **Primal Fear** •974

223

I'm no lawyer. All a lawyer cares about is the law.

Orson Welles as Hank Quinlan in **Touch of Evil** •975

As a matter of law, the truth of your story is irrelevant. We have no knowledge the story is false, therefore, we're absent malice.

John Harkins as Davidek, the lawyer, in **Absence of Malice** •976

You don't understand how I feel! I'm standing there with my pants down and my crotch hung out for the world to see and three guys are sticking it to me, a bunch of other guys are yelling and clapping and you're standing there telling me that that's the best you can do? *Jodie Foster as Sarah Tobias in* **The Accused** •977

Good and evil, right and wrong, were invented for the ordinary, average man, the inferior man, because he needs them. *John Dall as Brandon in* **Rope** •978

There was no way in all the world I could have known that murder sometimes can smell like honeysuckle. *Fred MacMurray as Walter Neff in* **Double Indemnity** •979

I'll take my chances against the law. You'll take yours against the sea.

Clark Gable as Fletcher Christian in **Mutiny on the Bounty** •980

A policeman's job is only easy in a police state. That's the whole point Captain – who's the Boss, the cop or the law?
Charlton Heston as Vargas in **Touch of Evil** •981

The rest of America don't mean a damn thing. You in Mississippi now.
Gailard Sartain as Sheriff Stuckey in **Mississippi Burning** •982

I'm your worst nightmare – a nigger with a badge.
Eddie Murphy as Reggie Hammond in **48 Hrs** •983

Serve the trust. Protect the innocent. Uphold the law.
Peter Weller as **Robocop** •984

Will: I know that I'm not smarter than you.
Lecter: Then how did you catch me?
Will: You had disadvantages.
Lecter: What disadvantages?
Will: You're insane.
William Petersen and Brian Cox in **Manhunter** •985

I have forsworn myself, I have broken every law I swore to defend, I have become what I beheld, and I'm content that I have done right.
Kevin Costner as Eliot Ness in **The Untouchables** •986

Anne: You're a cop for God's sake, you're supposed to uphold the law, but instead you bend it and twist it and sell it. I saw you take that bribe and resist arrest and tamper with evidence and perjure yourself under oath.
Remy: Don't forget I ran a red light too!
Anne: You still think it's funny, don't you? Why don't you just face it, Remy? You're not one of the good guys anymore.
Ellen Barkin and Dennis Quaid in **The Big Easy** •987

In Mexico, law enforcement is an entrepreneurial activity.
Miguel Ferrer as Ruiz in **Traffic** •988

Ray: Hey sugarfoot! How do you like your new place?
Ruiz: This is not what my lawyers negotiated.
Montel: Fuck your lawyers. You aren't getting any cappuccino or Biscotti either. You don't like it, call 1-800-CRIMINAL.
Ruiz meets some entrepreneurs (Luiz Guzman & Don Cheadle) in **Traffic** •989

Wilma, I promise you – whatever scum did this, not one man on this force will rest one minute until he's behind bars. Now, let's grab a bite to eat.

Leslie Nielsen as Frank Drebin in **Naked Gun** •990

The James Bond film formula is: think of a theme park with ten great rides and no waiting.

John Patterson •991

Good to see you Mr. Bond. Things have been awfully dull around here. I hope we're going to see some gratuitous sex and violence. *Alec McCowen as Q in* **Never Say Never Again** •992

I think you're a sexist, misogynist dinosaur. A relic of the Cold War, who's boyish charms, though wasted on me, obviously appealed to the young lady I sent out to evaluate you.

Judi Dench as M in **GoldenEye** •993

Bond: Who would pay $1m to have me killed?
M: Jealous husbands, outraged chefs, humiliated tailors — the list is endless.

Roger Moore and Bernard Miles in **The Man With The Golden Gun** •994

If I want sarcasm I'll speak to my children.

Judi Dench as the new M in **Goldeneye** •995

Roebuck: With all due respect, M, sometimes
I don't think you've got the balls for this job.
M: Perhaps, but the advantage is I don't have
to think with them all the time.

*Geoffrey Palmer as the Admiral
and Judi Dench in* **Tomorrow Never Dies** •996

Bond: Forgive me father for I have sinned.
Q: That's putting it mildly, 007!

*Roger Moore meets Desmond Llewellyn
in a Confessional in* **For Your Eyes Only** •997

Bond: You know, you're cleverer than you look.
Q: Still, better than looking cleverer than you are.

Brosnan and John Cleese sparring in **Die Another Day** •998

Need I remind you, 007, that you have a
license to kill, not to break traffic laws.
Desmond Llewellyn as Q in **GoldenEye** •999

Natalya Simonova: You destroy every vehicle you get into?
Bond: Standard operating procedure. Boys with toys.
Izabella Scorupco and Brosnan in **GoldenEye** •1000

Flattery will get you nowhere, but don't stop trying.
Lois Maxwell as Miss Moneypenny to Bond in **Dr No** •1001

Bond: Moneypenny, what gives?
Moneypenny: Me, given an ounce of encouragement.
Connery and Lois Maxwell as Moneypenny in **Dr No** •1002

Honey: Are you looking for shells too?
Bond: No, I'm just looking. *A bikini-clad Ursula Andress and Sean Connery in* **Dr No** •1003

Pussy: My name is Pussy Galore.
Bond: I must be dreaming.
Honor Blackman and Connery in **Goldfinger** •1004

Plenty: Hi, I'm Plenty.
Bond: Of course you are.
Lana Wood as Plenty O'Toole and Connery as Bond in **Diamonds Are Forever** •1005

229

I like a girl in a bikini.
No concealed weapons.

Christopher Lee as Scaramanga, talking about a scantily-clad
Britt Ekland in **The Man With The Golden Gun** •1006

I know all about you – sex for dinner, death for breakfast.

Rosamund Pike as Miranda Frost in **Die Another Day** •1007

Elektra: You could have had the world.
Bond: The world is not enough.
Elektra: Foolish sentiment.
Bond: Family motto.

Sophie Marceau and Pierce Brosnan
in **The World Is Not Enough** •1008

We have all the time in the world.

Bond (George Lazenby) to Diana Rigg as Tracy in **On Her Majesty's Secret**
Service; *she has just been shot.* •1009

World domination. Same old dream. Our asylums are
full of people who think they're Napoleon or God.

Connery as Bond to Dr No •1010

Unfortunately, I misjudged you. You are just
a stupid policeman whose luck has run out.

Joseph Wiseman as **Dr No** •1011

Choose your next witticism carefully, Mr Bond, it may be your last.

Gert Frobe as **Goldfinger** •1012

Bond: You expect me to talk?
Goldfinger: No, Mr Bond, I expect you to die.

Connery and Gert Frobe in **Goldfinger** •1013

Blofeld: Allow me to introduce myself. I am Ernst Stavro Blofeld.
They told me you were assassinated in Hong Kong.
Bond: Yes, this is my second life.
Blofeld: You only live twice, Mr Bond.

Donald Pleasance and Connery in **You Only Live Twice** •1014

Mr Bond is indeed a very rare breed. Soon to be made extinct.

Louis Jourdan as Kamal Khan in **Octopussy** •1015

You must admit, Mr Bond, that I am now, undeniably, the man with the golden gun. *Christopher Lee as Scaramanga in* **The Man With The Golden Gun** •1016

Jack Wade: Ex-KGB type. Tough mother.
Big guy with a limp. Name's Zukovsky.
Bond: Valentin Dmitrovic Zukovsky?
Wade: Yeah, you know him?
Bond: I gave him the limp.
Joe Don Baker and Brosnan in **GoldenEye** •1017

Oh, please, James, put it away. It's insulting to think I haven't anticipated your every move.
Sean Bean as former 006, Alec Trevelyan, in **GoldenEye** •1018

I think he got the point.
Bond, after shooting Varga (Philip Locke) with a harpoon in **Thunderball** •1019

Oh, he blew a fuse.
Connery, after Odd-job electrocutes himself in **Goldfinger** •1020

As you said, he had a pressing engagement.
Connery, having seen a villain crushed in a car in **Goldfinger** •1021

She's had her kicks.
Connery, after killing Rosa Klebb, she of the poisoned boots, in **From Russia With Love** •1022

Do I look like the sort of man who'd make trouble?
Connery in **Never Say Never Again** •1023

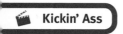

We came, we saw, we kicked it's ass!
Bill Murray as Venkman in **Ghostbusters** •1024

Hasta La Vista, baby.
Arnold Schwarzenegger in **Terminator 2: Judgment Day** •1025

You're terminated, fucker!
Linda Hamilton as Sarah O'Connor in **Terminator** •1026

Consider that a divorce!
Arnold Schwarzenegger as Douglas Quaid,
shooting his wife in **Total Recall.** •1027

Killian: You bastard! Drop dead!
Ben: I don't do requests.
Richard Dawson and Arnie in **The Running Man** •1028

Yippee-ki-yay, motherfucker.
Bruce Willis as John McClane in **Die Hard** •1029

That's a real badge. I'm a real cop.
And this is a real, firing gun.

Mel Gibson as Riggs in **Lethal Weapon** •1030

Belloq: Jones, do you realise what the Ark is? It's a transmitter. It's
a radio for speaking to God. And it's within my reach.
Indy: You wanna talk to God? Let's go see him together.

Paul Freeman and Harrison Ford in **Raiders of the Lost Ark** •1031

Listen. Since I've met you I've nearly
been incinerated, drowned, shot at,
and chopped into fish bait.

Harrison Ford in **Indiana Jones and The Last Crusade** •1032

You're not a cook.

*Erika Eleniak as Jordan stating the obvious
to Steven Siegel in* **Under Siege** •1033

We will not abandon Merry and Pippin to torment and death.
Not while we have strength left. Leave all that can be spared
behind. We travel light. Let's hunt some Orc.

Viggo Mortensen as Aragorn in **Lord of The Rings: Fellowship of the Ring** •1034

We are now up against live, hostile targets. So, if Little Red Riding Hood should show up with a bazooka and a bad attitude, I expect you to chin the bitch. *Sean Pertwee as Sgt Harry Wells in* **Dog Soldiers** •1035

I know that I have put you through hell, and I know that I have been one rough pecker. But from here on, you are all in my cool book. *George Clooney as Seth in* **From Dusk 'Til Dawn** •1036

Ever notice how you come across somebody once in a while you shouldn't have fucked with? That's me.
Clint Eastwood as octagenarian hard-case Walt Kowalski in **Gran Torino** •1037

A good fight should be like a small play, but played seriously. When the opponent expands, I contract. When he contracts, I expand. And when the opportunity presents itself, I do not hit. It hits all by itself. *Bruce Lee talking about*
Enter The Dragon •1038

Bless me, Father, for I have just killed quite a few men.
Antonio Banderas as El Mariachi in **Desperado** •1039

OK, Vampire Anatomy 101; crosses and running water
don't do dick so you forget what you've seen
in the movies. You use a stake, silver or sunlight.
Wesley Snipes as **Blade** •1040

President: What do you think, Marsha?
First Lady: Kick the crap out of 'em.
Jack Nicholson and Glenn Close in **Mars Attacks** •1041

Hello. My name is Inigo Montoya.
You killed my father. Prepare to die.
Mandy Patinkin as Inigo Montoya in **The Princess Bride** •1042

At my signal, unleash hell.
Russell Crowe as Maximus in **Gladiator** •1043

This picture is dedicated to all the beautiful women in the world who have shot their husbands full of holes out of pique. *Opening line from* **Roxie Hart,** *1942* •1044

That is the kind of woman that makes civilizations topple. *Kathleen Howard as Miss Bragg, on Barbara Stanwyck in* **Ball of Fire** •1045

You've been trying to make a tramp out of me ever since you've known me.

Lana Turner as Cora Smith in **The Postman Always Rings Twice** •1046

I get the idea. She was a tramp from a long line of tramps.

Fred MacMurray as Walter Neff talking about Barbara Stanwyck in **Double Indemnity** •1047

I loved you, Walter, and I hated him. But I wasn't going to do anything about it. Not until I met you. You planned the whole thing. I only wanted him dead. *Barbara Stanwyck as Phyllis in* **Double Indemnity** •1048

You're slumming and I don't go for slummers. You think you're too good for me – well it so happens I think I'm too good for you. *Alan Ladd to Veronica Lake in* **The Glass Key** •1049

I used to have a speech impediment. I couldn't say no.
Annabella Sciorra as Susan in **The Hard Way** •1050

You're just another good-looking, sweet talking,
charm-oozing, fuck-happy fella with nothing to offer
but some dialogue. Dialogue's cheap in Hollywood,
Ben. Why don't you run outside and jerk yourself
a soda? *Annette Bening as Virginia in* **Bugsy** •1051

Don't fuck with me fellas! This
ain't my first time at the rodeo.
Faye Dunaway as Joan Crawford in **Mommie Dearest** •1052

It took more than one man to change my name
to Shanghai Lily. *Marlene Dietrich as Lily*
in **Shanghai Express** •1053

I can never get a zipper to close. Maybe that stands for
something, what do you think? *Rita Hayworth as* **Gilda** •1054

If I'd been a ranch, they would
have named me the Bar Nothing.
Rita Hayworth as **Gilda** •1055

I've been rich and I've been poor. Believe me, rich is better.
Gloria Grahame as Debby Marsh in **The Big Heat** •1056

I first played a gangster's moll on Broadway in *On the Spot* which led to *Little Caesar* in Hollywood. Then all those wisecracking, heart of gold blondes. I played so many bad girls that when I went to London in 1937, the headline read, "Tough Baby Arrives." *Glenda Farrell* •1057

I've succeeded because I've always known I was born to dominate your sex and avenge my own. *Glenn Close as Marquise de Merteuil in* **Dangerous Liaisons** •1058

Sometimes you have to be a high-riding bitch to survive. Sometimes being a bitch is all a woman has to hold on to. *Judy Parfitt as Vera in* **Dolores Claiborne** •1059

It's the good girls who keep diaries. The bad girls never have the time. *Tallulah Bankhead* •1060

I'm not bad, I'm just drawn that way.
Kathleen Turner as the voice of Jessica Rabbit in **Who Framed Roger Rabbit?** •1061

There aren't any hard women – just soft men. *Bette Davis* •1062

The chicks are packed!
Marcelino Sanchez as Rembrandt in **The Warriors** •1063

Emma: I'm going to kill you.
Vienna: I know. If I don't kill you first.
Mercedes McCambridge and Joan Crawford in **Johnny Guitar** •1064

These guys are about as much fun as a tax audit.
Mary Elizabeth Mastrantonio as Lindsay takes a dim view of Navy Seals in **The Abyss** •1065

I wanna buy a gun… one that'll take the head off a honky at twenty paces! *Gail Neely as Mama Washington in* **Surf Nazis Must Die** •1066

Well, my hair is coming down.
Geena Davis as Thelma in **Thelma and Louise** •1067

Take all the cash out of that drawer and put it in a paper bag. You're gonna have an amazing story to tell all your friends. If not, you'll have a tag on your toe. You decide.
Geena Davis as Thelma in **Thelma and Louise** •1068

Life's a bitch. Now so am I. •1069

I don't know about you, Miss Kitty, but I feel so much yummier. •1070

You poor guys. Always confusing your pistols with your privates. •1071

You're catnip to a girl like me. Handsome, dazed, and to die for. You're the second man who killed me this week, but I've got seven lives left. •1072

Michelle Pfeiffer as Catwoman in **Batman Returns**

Get away from her, you bitch!
Sigourney Weaver as Ripley in **Aliens** •1073

Don't call me babe!
Pamela Anderson in **Barb Wire** •1074

You gotta think about it like the first time you got laid.
You gotta go: "Daddy, are you sure this is right?"
Lori Petty as **Tank Girl** •1075

Look, if you want to torture me, spank me, lick me, do it. But if this poetry shit continues just shoot me now please. *Lori Petty as* **Tank Girl** •1076

You just contact the mayor's office.
He has a special signal he shines in the
sky; it's in the shape of a giant cock.

*Hit-Girl (Chloe Moretz) explains how she can be
contacted in case of emergency in* **Kick-Ass** •1077

Remember where you are — this is Thunderdome, and death is listening, and will take the first man that screams.

Tina Turner as Auntie Entity in **Mad Max Beyond Thunderdome** •1078

Violence in real life is terrible; violence in the movies can be cool. It's just another colour to work with. *Quentin Tarantino.* •1079

I steal from every single movie ever made. I love it — if my work has anything it's that I'm taking this from this and that from that and mixing them together. *Tarantino* •1080

If I hadn't wanted to make movies, I'd have done something that I would have gone to jail for.

Tarantino •1081

Seeing Bambi's mum get killed is probably more frightening than anything in *Reservoir Dogs.*
Tarantino talking bollocks •1082

If you're talking like a bitch, I'm gonna slap you like a bitch. *Michael Madsen as Mr Blonde* •1083

Mr Pink: How about if I'm Mr. Purple? That sounds good to me, I'll be Mr. Purple.
Joe: You're not Mr. Purple. Some guy on some other job is Mr. Purple. You're Mr. Pink!
Mr White: Who cares what your name is?
Mr Pink: Yeah that's easy for you to say, you're Mr. White, you have a cool sounding name. All right look if it's no big deal to be Mr. Pink, do you wanna trade?
Steve Buscemi, Lawrence Tierney and Harvey Keitel in **Reservoir Dogs** •1084

Are you gonna bark all day, little doggie, or are you gonna bite? *Michael Madsen as Mr Blonde* •1085

You're acting like a first year fucking thief. I'm acting like a professional. *Steve Buscemi as Mr Pink* •1086

Look, I'm not stupid. It's the Big Man's wife. I'm gonna sit across from her, chew my food with my mouth closed, laugh at her fucking jokes, and that's it. *John Travolta as Vincent in* **Pulp Fiction** •1087

Vincent: Which one is Trudi? The one with all the shit on her face? Lance: No, that's Jody. That's my wife.

Travolta puts his foot in it with Eric Stoltz in **Pulp Fiction** •1088

Normally, both your asses would be dead as fucking fried chicken, but you happen to pull this shit while I'm in a transitional period so I don't wanna kill you, I wanna help you. *Samuel L Jackson as Jules in* **Pulp Fiction** •1089

Pumpkin: Alright, everybody be cool, this is a robbery!
Yolanda: Any of you fucking pricks move, and I'll execute every motherfucking last one of ya!
Tim Roth and Amanda Plummer in **Pulp Fiction** •1090

AK-47. When you absolutely, positively got to kill every motherfucker in the room, accept no substitutes. *Samuel L Jackson as Ordell in* **Jackie Brown** •1091

Jackie can tell me any story that comes into her pretty little head, just so long as at the end of that story she hands me my motherfucking money. *Samuel L Jackson as Ordell in* **Jackie Brown** •1092

Ordell: See, that shit works my nerves, you being all buddy-buddy with that motherfucker.
Jackie: If I wasn't so buddy-buddy with that motherfucker, none of this would work.
Samuel L Jackson and Pam Grier in **Jackie Brown** •1093

Ordell: That shit'll rob you of your ambitions.
Melanie: Not if your ambition is to get high and watch TV.
Samuel L Jackson and Bridget Fonda in **Jackie Brown** •1094

Shut your raggedy-ass up, and sit the fuck down!

Pam Grier as **Jackie Brown** •1095

It's mercy, compassion, and forgiveness I lack; not rationality.

Uma Thurman as **The Bride** in **Kill Bill Vol 1** •1096

Budd: You're telling me she cut through eighty-eight
bodyguards before she got to O-Ren?
Bill: Nah, there weren't really eighty-eight of them.
They just called themselves "The Crazy 88."
Budd: How come?
Bill: I don't know. I guess they thought it sounded cool.

Michael Madsen and David Carradine in **Kill Bill Vol 2** •1097

Elle Driver: That's right. I killed your master. And now I'm
gonna kill you, with your own sword, no less, which in the
very immediate future, will become… my sword.
The Bride: Bitch, you don't have a future.

Daryl Hannah and Uma Thurman in **Kill Bill vol 2** •1098

The Bride: You and I have unfinished business.
Bill: Baby, you ain't kidding. *Uma Thurman and David Carradine*
in **Kill Bill vol 2** •1099

I don't make movies that
bring people together. *Tarantino* •1100

To a new world of Gods and Monsters!

Ernest Thesiger as Pretorius in **The Bride of Frankenstein** •1101

We'll begin with a reign of terror – a few murders here and there.
Murders of great men; murders of little men – just to show we
make no distinction. *Claude Rains as* **The Invisible Man** •1102

I am the monster that breathing men would kill.
I am Dracula. *Gary Oldman in* **Bram Stoker's Dracula** •1103

Listen to them, the children of the
night. What music they make.

Bela Lugosi as the Count in **Dracula** •1104

I give you life eternal. Everlasting love. The power
of the storm, and the beasts of the earth. Walk
with me… to be my loving
wife… forever. *Gary Oldman in* **Bram Stoker's Dracula** •1105

I'm just a hair away from being a serial killer.
Dennis Hopper •1106

Have you ever seen blood in the moonlight, Will?
It appears quite black. *Brian Cox as Hannibal Lecter*
*in **Manhunter** •1107*

A census taker once tried to test me. I ate his
liver with some fava beans and a nice chianti.
*Anthony Hopkins as Hannibal Lecter in **Silence of the Lambs** •1108*

Death has come to your little town, Sheriff. Now you
can either ignore it, or you can help me to stop it.
*Donald Pleasence as Dr Sam Loomis in **Hallowe'en** •1109*

Casey: What do you want?
Voice on phone: To see what your insides look like.
*Drew Barrymore and caller in **Scream** •1110*

Mother — what's the phrase? — isn't
quite herself today. *Anthony Perkins as Norman in **Psycho** •1111*

It's the so-called normal guys who always let you down.
Sickos never scare me. At least they're committed.
*Michelle Pfeiffer as Catwoman in **Batman Returns** •1112*

H-A-T-E. It was with this left hand that old brother Cain struck the blow that laid *his* brother low.
L-O-V-E. You see these fingers, dear hearts?
These fingers have veins that run straight to the soul of man – the right hand, friends, the hand of love.

Robert Mitchum as the Preacher in **The Night of the Hunter** •1113

There is a power of evil in that film, in the fabric of the film itself.

Billy Graham, preacher, on **The Exorcist** •1114

There is a pain beyond pain, an agony so intense it shocks the mind into instant beauty.

Vincent Price as Professor Jarrod in **House of Wax** •1115

All I did was take pictures…

Robin Williams as Sy Parrish in **One Hour Photo** •1116

I'm your number one fan.

Kathy Bates as Annie Wilkes in **Misery** •1117

I'm not going to be ignored!

Glenn Close as Alex in **Fatal Attraction** •1118

I do wish we could chat longer but I'm having an old friend for dinner.
Anthony Hopkins as Hannibal Lecter in **Silence of the Lambs** •1119

My mother told me to never do this.

C Thomas Howell as Jim Halsey, picking up Rutger Hauer in **Hitcher**. *His mum was right.* •1120

Some places are like people.
Some shine and some don't.
Scatman Crothers as Hallorann in **The Shining** •1121

There is something down there. Something not us. *Mary*
Elizabeth Mastrantonio as Lindsay in **The Abyss** •1122

This isn't a dream, this is really happening.

Mia Farrow as Rosemary, being raped by the devil in **Rosemary's Baby** •1123

253

We're gonna be french fries! Human french fries!

Susan Lanier as Brenda Carter in **The Hills Have Eyes** •1124

You gonna write us a happy ending, Heather?

Joshua Leonard in **The Blair Witch Project** •1125

Well, Clarice, have the lambs stopped screaming?

Anthony Hopkins as Hannibal Lecter in **Silence of the Lambs** •1126

254

A lot of people with names like Zircona, Placenta and Tampon crawling through air vents. *Mark Lamarr dismisses sci-fi movies.* •1127

Have you ever danced with the devil in the pale moonlight? *Jack Nicholson as The Joker in* **Batman** •1128

I spent a lot of time being scared for you. And I heard you were back. But the man I loved, the man who vanished never came back. *Katie Holmes as Rachel in* **Batman Begins** •1129

You're just jealous because I'm a genuine freak and you have to wear a mask.
Danny DeVito as The Penguin in **Batman Returns** •1130

Do I really look like a guy with a plan? You know what I am? I'm a dog chasing cars. I wouldn't know what to do with one if I caught it. You know, I just… do things. The mob has plans, the cops have plans, Gordon's got plans. You know, they're schemers. Schemers trying to control their little worlds. I'm not a schemer. I try to show the schemers how pathetic their attempts to control things really are.
Heath Ledger as The Joker in **The Dark Knight**•1131

Close your eyes and tap your heels together three times. And think to yourself, "There's no place like home."

Billie Burke as Glinda, The Witch of the South, in **The Wizard of Oz** •1132

It would be so nice if something made sense for a change.

Kathryn Beaumont as Alice in **Alice In Wonderland** •1133

I shall stay until the wind changes. *Julie Andrews as* **Mary Poppins** •1134

Elliott: He's a man from outer space and we're taking him to his spaceship.
Greg: Well can't he just beam up?
Elliott: This is reality, Greg.

Henry Thomas and KC Martel in **E.T.** •1135

Hammond: When they opened Disneyland in 1956, nothing worked. Malcolm: Yes, but John, if the Pirates of the Caribbean breaks down, the pirates don't eat the tourists.

Richard Attenborough and Jeff Goldblum in **Jurassic Park** •1136

Harding: I'll be back in five or six days.
Malcolm: No, you'll be back in five or six pieces!

Julianne Moore and Jeff Goldblum in **The Lost World** •1137

I am a Vulcan. I have no ego to bruise.

Leonard Nimoy as Spock in **Star Trek II: The Wrath of Khan** •1138

I am Connor MacLeod of the Clan MacLeod.
I was born in 1518 in the village of Glenfinnan
on the shores of Loch Shiel. And I am immortal.

Christophe Lambert in **Highlander** •1139

Put up your arms and all your flippers.

Tommy Lee Jones as Agent K in **Men In Black** •1140

You should've bargained, Jabba.

Harrison Ford as Han Solo in **Return of the Jedi** •1141

Decrucify the angel or I'll melt your face!

Jane Fonda as **Barbarella** •1142

257

It's OK, I'm still dad. It's just that something is happening to me I can't describe.

Richard Dreyfuss as Roy Neary in **Close Encounters of the Third Kind** •1143

Spoon Boy: Do not try and bend the spoon, that's impossible. Instead, only try and realise the truth.
Neo: What truth?
Spoon Boy: There is no spoon.

Rowan Witt and Keanu Reeves in **The Matrix** •1144

Human beings are a disease, a cancer of this planet; you are a plague and we are the cure.

Hugo Weaving as Agent Smith in **The Matrix** •1145

I'm a Libra. What sign are you? No wait, don't tell me — I bet you're an Ares, aren't you? *Jessica Lange talks star signs to* **King Kong.** •1146

The fool, the meddling idiot. As though his ape's brain could contain the secrets of the Krell.

Walter Pidgeon as Morbius in **Forbidden Planet** •1147

258

The world you live in is just a sugar-coated topping.
There is another world beneath it. The real world.

Wesley Snipes as **Blade** •1148

The report read, "Routine retirement
of a replicant." That didn't make me
feel any better about shooting a woman
in the back. *Harrison Ford as Deckard in* **Blade Runner** •1149

Does believing you're the last sane man on the planet make you crazy? 'Cause if that's the case, maybe I am.

Will Smith as Spooner in **I, Robot** •1150

It's going to be blood for blood and by the gallon. These are the old days, the bad days, the all-or-nothing days. They're back!

Mickey Rourke as Marv in **Sin City** •1151

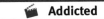

Remember; alcohol equals puke equals smelly mess equals nobody likes you.
Adam Sandler as Robbie in **The Wedding Singer** •1216

I always start around noon — in case it gets dark early.
Peggy Lee as Rose Hopkins in **Pete Kelly's Blues** •1217

I distrust a man that says "when". If he's got to be careful not to drink too much, it's because he's not to be trusted when he does.
Sydney Greenstreet to Humphrey Bogart in **The Maltese Falcon** •1218

I demand to have some booze!
Richard E. Grant as Withnail in **Withnail and I** •1219

Gimme whisky… ginger ale on the side. And don't be stingy, baby.
Greta Garbo as **Anna Christie** •1220

Don't drink alone, Scarlett. People always find out and it ruins the reputation.
Clark Gable as Rhett Butler in **Gone With The Wind** •1221

I'll admit I may have seen better days, but I'm still not to be had for the price of a cocktail, like a salted peanut.
Bette Davis as Margo in **All About Eve** •1222

Jefty Robbins: Have a drink. I kept the bar open for you.
Lily Stevens: Sure, I could use a little cooking sherry.
Richard Widmark & Ida Lupino in **Road House** •1223

She was a charming middle-aged lady with a face like a bucket of mud.
I gave her a drink. She was a gal who'd take a drink if she had to knock
you down to get the bottle. *Dick Powell as Phillip Marlowe in* **Farewell, My Lovely** •1224

I never drink when I fly.
Christopher Reeve as **Superman** •1225

We want the finest wines available to
humanity. We want them here, and
we want them now! *Richard E. Grant
as Withnail in* **Withnail and I** •1226

I have made a discovery; champagne
is more fun to drink than goat's milk.
Cyd Charisse as Ninotchka in **Silk Stockings** •1227

Hey, did you ever try dunking a potato chip in champagne? It's real crazy!
Marilyn Monroe as The Girl in **The Seven Year Itch** •1228

I drink only beer and a little wine. Champagne?
Oh no. Champagne I only bathe in. *Hedy Lamarr* •1229

You see, drinking is really a matter of algebraic ratios. How drunk you get is dependent on how much alcohol you consume in relation to your total body weight. You see my point? It's not that you had a lot to drink. It's just you're too skinny. *John Candy as Freddie to a comatose Tom Hanks in* **Splash!** •1230

Of course I'm drunk. You don't really expect me to teach this when I'm sober? *Michael Caine as Frank Bryant in* **Educating Rita** •1231

I've tried Buddhism, Scientology, Numerology, Transcendental Meditation, Qabbala, tai-chi, feng shui and Deepak Chopra but I find straight gin works best. *Phyllis Diller* •1232

I meditate, I do yoga and I have a lot of friends who are healers. I go to psychics and numerologists. And if none of that works, I go buy a chocolate bar and a bottle of cognac. *Susan Strasberg* •1233

What I'm trying to say is, I'm not a drinker – I'm a drunk.

Ray Milland as Don Birman in **The Lost Weekend** •1234

Look, sweetheart, I can drink you under any goddamn table
you want, so don't worry about me.   *Elizabeth Taylor as Martha in*
Who's Afraid of Virginia Woolf •1235

You know, I used to think the world looked
better for a glass of whisky. It doesn't
Arthur O'Connell as Parnell McCarthy in **Anatomy of a Murder** •1236

Anyone who stayed drunk twenty five years as
I did would have to be in trouble. Hell, I used to
take two-week lunch hours. *Spencer Tracy* •1237

The trouble with the world is that everybody in it is three drinks behind.

Humphrey Bogart •1238

I tried to keep away from these things. I tried. Honestly, I tried.
I hadn't had a stitch of them on for nearly a week, and then I
couldn't take it anymore. I had to put it on or go out of my mind.
Ed Wood battles his fluffy sweater addiction in **Glen or Glenda** •1239

265

I'm sure I'd feel much worse if I wasn't under heavy sedation.
Michael McKean as David St Hubbins in **This Is Spinal Tap** •1240

Dylan: Chill out guys, I've got something stashed that just might help.
Brian: Dylan, we don't have time to indulge in recreational activities…
Bill Nighy and Jim Broadbent (voices) as Dylan and Brian in **The Magic Roundabout** •1241

I've got pot, I've got acid, I've got LSD cubes. I'm probably the hippest guy around here. I'm so hip, it hurts!
Peter Sellers as Harold Fine in **I Love You, Alice B Toklas** •1242

We had two bags of grass, seventy-five pellets of mescaline, five sheets of high-powered blotter-acid, a salt-shaker half full of cocaine, and a whole galaxy of multi-coloured uppers, downers, screamers, laughers; also a quart of tequila, a quart of rum, a case of beer, a pint of raw ether, and two dozen amyls. But the only thing that worried me was the ether.
Johnny Depp as Raoul Duke in **Fear and Loathing in Las Vegas** •1243

See you Monday. We'll be talking about Freud and why he did enough cocaine to kill a small horse. *Robin Williams as Sean in* **Good Will Hunting** •1244

Who needs reasons when you've got heroin?
Ewan McGregor as Renton in **Trainspotting** •1245

Right, here's the plan. First, we go in there and get wrecked, then we eat a pork pie, then we drop some Surmontil-50's each. That way we'll miss out on Monday and come up smiling Tuesday morning.

Richard E Grant as Withnail in **Withnail And I** •1246

I've smoked two joints in my life. Someone handed me cocaine at a party in a dish with a gold spoon. I thought it was Sweet 'n' Low and put it in my coffee. *Shirley MacLaine* •1247

Winston: You went out six hours ago to buy a money counter and you come back with a semi-conscious Gloria and a bag of fertilizer. Alarm bells are ringing, Willie.

Willie: We need fertilizer Winston.

Winston: Mmmhmm. We also need a money counter. This money's got to be out by Thursday, I'm buggered if I'm gonna count it. Just make sure if you do need to buy sodding fertilizer you could be a bit more subtle.

Willie: What do you mean?

Winston: We grow copious amounts of ganja, yah? And you're carrying a wasted girl and a bag of fertilizer. You don't look like your average horti-fucking-culturalist! That's what I mean Willie.

Steven Macintosh & Charles Forbes in **Lock, Stock and Two Smoking Barrels** •1248

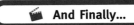

Cigarette me, big boy.

Ginger Rogers as Puff in **Young Man of Manhattan** •1249

I want to be alone…

Garbo in **Grand Hotel** •1250

Well, here's another nice mess you've gotten me into!
Time honoured phrase of Oliver Hardy to Stan Laurel •1251

Toto, I have a feeling we're not in Kansas anymore.

Judy Garland in **The Wizard of Oz** •1252

Scarlett: Where shall I go? Where shall I go?
Rhett: Frankly, my dear, I don't give a damn.

Vivien Leigh and Clark Gable in **Gone With The Wind** •1253

Major Strasser has been shot. Round up the usual suspects.
Claude Rains as Louis Renault in **Casablanca** •1254

You've been a long way away.
Thank you for coming back to me.

Cyril Raymond as Fred in **Brief Encounter** •1255

Fasten your seat belts. It's going to be a bumpy night.
*Bette Davis as Margo in **All About Eve*** •1256

I always get the fuzzy end of the lollipop.
*Marilyn Monroe as Sugar Cane in **Some Like It Hot*** •1257

Nothing is written.
*Peter O'Toole as **Lawrence of Arabia*** •1258

Please sir, I want some more.
*Mark Lester as Oliver Twist in **Oliver!*** •1259

You're only supposed to blow the bloody doors off!
*Michael Caine as Charlie Croker in **The Italian Job*** •1260

I'm gonna make him an offer he can't refuse.
*Marlon Brando as Don Corleone in **The Godfather*** •1261

You're gonna need a bigger boat!
*Roy Scheider as Martin Brody in **Jaws*** •1262

The force will be with you – always.
Alec Guinness as Obi-Wan Kenobi to Luke Skywalker in **Star Wars** •1263

Superman: Easy, miss, I've got you.
Lois Lane: You've got me? Who's got you?
Christopher Reeve and Margot Kidder in **Superman** •1264

I love the smell of napalm in the morning… it smells like victory.
Robert Duvall as Lt Col Kilgore in **Apocalypse Now** •1265

Alright, but apart from the sanitation, medicine, education, wine, public order, irrigation, roads, the fresh water system and public health, what have the Romans ever done for us? *John Cleese as Reg in* **The Life of Brian** •1266

Did you ever do it to Ravel's *Bolero*? *Bo Derek as Jenny in* **10** •1267

We're on a mission from God.

Dan Aykroyd and John Belushi in **The Blues Brothers** •1268

Heeeere's Johnny!

Nicholson as Jack Torrance in **The Shining** •1269

Snakes. Why did it have to be snakes?!

Harrison Ford as Indiana Jones in **Raiders of the Lost Ark** •1270

I'll be back.

Arnie as **The Terminator** •1271

My mama always said, life is like a box of chocolates. You never know what you're gonna get.

Tom Hanks as **Forrest Gump** •1272

I see dead people.

Haley Joel Osment as Cole Sear in **The Sixth Sense** •1273

273

Hang on a minute, lads, I've got a great idea...
Michael Caine as Charlie Croker in **The Italian Job** •1274

So this is where you live. Oh, mother will love it up here. *Grace Kelly as Frances Stevens in* **To Catch A Thief** •1275

Jerry: We can't get married at all... I'm a man.
Osgood E Fielding III: Well, nobody's perfect.
Jack Lemmon and Joe E Brown in **Some Like It Hot** •1276

Well, thank you, Harvey, I prefer you too.
James Stewart to Harvey, the imaginary rabbit, in **Harvey.** •1277

Louis, I think this is the beginning of a beautiful friendship.
Bogart as Rick to Claude Rains in **Casablanca** •1278

Roslyn: How do you find your way back in the dark?
Gay: Just head for that big star straight on. The highway's under it. It'll take us right home.
Marilyn Monroe and Clark Gable in **The Misfits.** *For both actors it was their final screen line. Gable was dead by the time the film was released and Monroe died the year after release.* •1279

Shut up and deal.

Shirley Maclaine, the last line in **The Apartment** •1280

I truly believe that happiness is possible… even when you're thirty-three and have a bottom the size of two bowling balls.

Renee Zellweger in **Bridget Jones: Edge of Reason** •1281

Give me a girl at an impressionable age, and she is mine for life.

Maggie Smith in **The Prime of Miss Jean Brodie** •1282

Eliza, where the devil are my slippers?

Rex Harrison as Henry Higgins in **My Fair Lady** •1283

I now pronounce you men and wives.

Ian Wolfe as Rev Elcott at the end of **Seven Brides For Seven Brothers** •1284

Take off the red shoes.

Moira Shearer as Victoria in **Red Shoes** •1285

Haven't got a sensible name, Calloway.
Joseph Cotten as Holly Martins in **The Third Man** •1286

He used to be a big shot.
Gladys George as Panama on James Cagney in **The Roaring Twenties** •1287

Mother of Mercy, is this the end of Rico?
Edward G. Robinson as the dying Rico in **Little Caesar** •1288

Oh no, it wasn't the airplanes. It was beauty killed the beast.
Robert Armstrong as Carl Denham in **King Kong** •1289

I was cured, all right.
Malcolm McDowell as Alex in **A Clockwork Orange** •1290

I don't know. I'd like to go home and I'd like to play with my dog.
Jodie Foster as Sarah Tobias in **The Accused** •1291

In spite of everything, I still believe that people are really good at heart.

Millie Perkins as Anne Frank in **The Diary of Anne Frank** •1292

I'm too old for this.

Danny Glover as Murtagh in **Lethal Weapon** •1293

I'll be right here. *Pat Welsh as the voice of* **E.T.** •1294

You be careful out among them English.

Jan Rubes as Amish elder, Eli Lapp, issuing a final warning to the departing Harrison Ford in **Witness** •1295

Nothing's forgiven.
Nothing.
Haing S. Ngor narrating as Dith Pran, **The Killing Fields** •1296

There's nothing else, just us, the cameras and those wonderful people out there in the dark. All right, Mr De Mille, I'm ready for my close-up.

Gloria Swanson as Norma Desmond in **Sunset Boulevard** •1297

Every one of you listening to my voice, tell the world. Tell this to everybody, wherever they are. Watch the skies, everywhere, keep looking. Keep watching the skies.

Douglas Spencer as Scatty in **The Thing** •1298

My friends, you have seen this incident based on sworn testimony. Can you prove that it didn't happen? Perhaps, on your way home, someone will tap you in the dark, and you will never know it, for they will be from Outer Space!

Final words, **Plan 9 From Outer Space** •1299

The world shall hear from me again.

Christopher Lee in **The Face of Fu Manchu** •1300

Educating Rita *1983* •234 •714 •1231 | Edward Scissorhands *1990* •118 | Election *1999* •387 | Elizabeth *1998* •291 | Emma *1996* •111 | Empire Strikes Back *1980* •384 •516 | Exorcist, The *1973* •1114 | Eyes Wide Shut *1999* •605 | Fabulous Baker Boys *1989* •640 | Face of Fu Manchu *1965* •1300 | Fan *1996* •357 | Farewell, My Lovely *1944* •1224 | Faster, Pussycat! Kill! Kill! *1965* •607 | Fatal Attraction *1987* •469 •1118 | Fear and Loathing in Las Vegas *1998* •1243 | Fever Pitch *1997* •392 | Fight Club *1999* •471 | Fish Called Wanda *1988* •719 | Flinstones *1994* •797 | Footlight Parade *1933* •688 | For Whom the Bell Tolls *1943* •435 | For Your Eyes Only *1981* •997 | Forbidden Planet *1956* •1147 | Forrest Gump *1994* •72 •1272 | Four Weddings And A Funeral *1984* •380 •521 | Frankie and Johnny *1991* •372 •528 | French Connection *1971* •915 | Frenzy *1972* •962 | Frida *2002* •502 | From Dusk 'Til Dawn *1996* •1036 | From Here to Eternity *1953* •533 | From Russia With Love *1963* •1022 | Frost/Nixon *2008* •281 | Full Monty *1997* •215 | Gandhi *1982* •181 •313 •314 | Gangs of New York *2002* •877 | Garden State *2004* •540 •662 | Genevieve *1953* •498 | Georgy Girl *1966* •311 | Get Carter *1971* •712 •924 | Get Shorty *1995* •647 | Ghostbusters *1984* •795 •1024 | Giant *1956* •404 | Gigi *1958* •338 | Gilda *1946* •1054 •1055 | Gladiator *2000* •929 •1043 | Glass Key *1942* •1049 | Glen or Glenda *1953* •1239 | Glengarry Glen Ross *1992* •726 | Go West *1940* •816 | Go West, Young Man *1936* •737 | Godafther II *1974* •881 | Godfather *1972* •1261 | GoldenEye *1995* •993 •995 •999 •1000 •1017 •1018 | Goldfinger *1964* •1004 •1012 •1013 •1020 •1021 | Gone In Sixty Seconds *2000* •360 •792 •938 | Gone With The Wind *1939* •442 •443 •1221 •1253 | Good Morning, Vietnam *1987* •276 •711 •786 | Good Will Hunting *1997* •320 •437 •1244 | Goodfellas *1990* •872 | Graduate *1967* •424 •425 •426 | Gran Torino *2008* •1037 | Grand Hotel *1932* •1250 | Grapes of Wrath *1940* •933 | Grease *1978* •606 | Great Dictator *1940* •318 | Greatest Show On Earth *1952* •401 •410 | Grifters *1990* •704 | Groundhog Day *1993* •785 | Guys and Dolls *1955* •556 | Hackers *1995* •301 •616 | Hallowe'en *1978* •1109 | Hangover, The *2009* •656 | Hannah and Her Sisters *1986* •670 | Happiness *1998* •174 | Hard Way *1991* •1050 | Harold and Maude *1972* •340 | Harriet The Spy *1996* •297 •728 | Harvey *1950* •1277 | Heartburn *1986* •577 •590 | Heat *1995* •887 | Heaven Can Wait *1978* •275 | Hedwig and the Angry Inch *2001* •654 | Hell's Angels *1930* •412 | High Fidelity *2000* •196 •794 | Highlander *1986* •1139 | Hilary and Jackie *1998* •321 | Hills Have Eyes *1977* •1124 | Hitcher *1986* •1120 | Hold Me, Thrill Me, Kiss Me *1992* •489 | Horse Feathers *1932* •803 •804

1989 •721 | **Tank Girl** *1995* •1075 •1076 | **Taxi Driver** *1931* •873 | **Team America: World Police** *2004* •773 | **Tender Trap** *1955* •559 | **Terminator** *1984* •1026 •1271 | **Terminator2: Judgment Day** *1991* •642 •917 •1025 | **That Darn Cat!** *1965* •26 | **Thelma and Louise** *1991* •463 •1067 •1068 | **There's A Girl In My Soup** *1970* •398 | **There's Something About Mary** *1998* •796 | **They Drive By Night** *1940* •411 | **Thin Man** *1934* •690 •941 | **Thing** *1951* •1298 | **Third Man** *1949* •286 •1286 | **This Is Spinal Tap** *1984* •86 •776 •777 •1240 | **Three Coins in the Fountain** *1954* •580 | **Three Men and A Baby** *1987* •618 | **Thunderball** *1965* •1019 | **Titanic** *1997* •65 •210 •568 | **To Catch A Thief** *1955* •406 •444 •1275 | **To Have and Have Not** *1944* •413 •897 •898 | **To Kill A Mockingbird** *1962* •334 •965 |

Tom Jones *1963* •400 •587 | **Tomorrow Never Dies** *1997* •996 | **Top Gun** *1981* •399 | **Total Recall** *1990* •1027 | **Touch of Evil** *1958* •975 •981 | **Toy Story** *1995* •420 | **Traffic** *2000* •988 •989 | **Trainspotting** *1996* •1245 | **Tropic Thunder** *2008* •778 | **True Lies** *1994* •927 | **Truly, Madly, Deeply** *1991* •524 | **Twelve Angry Men** *1957* •966 | **Twilight Saga: New Moon** *2009* •535 | **Twin Peaks** *1992* •475 | **Twin Town** *1997* •649 | **Tycoon** *1947* •66 | **Unbearable Lightness of Being** *1988* •391 | **Under Siege** *1992* •1033 | **Untouchables** *1987* •883 •986

Usual Suspects *1995* •888 | **V.I.Warshawski** *1991* •614 | **Velvet Goldmine** *1998* •457 | **Verdict** *1982* •967 •968 •969 | **Wall Street** *1987* •277 | **Warriors** *1979* •923 •1063 | **Way of Gun** *2000* •598 •889 | **Wayne's World** *1992* •208 •389 •694 | **Wedding Singer** *1998* •1216 | **When Harry Met Sally** *1989* •364 •604 | **White Heat** *1949* •202 | **White Men Can't Jump** *1992* •344 •717 | **Who Framed Roger Rabbit?** *1988* •1061 | **Whole Nine Yards** *2000* •944 | **Who's Afraid of Virginia Woolf** *1966* •552 •554 •1235 | **Wild At Heart** *1990* •300 •302 •468 | **Wild One** *1953* •298 | **Wish You Were Here** *1983* •209 | **Withnail and I** *1986* •1219 •1226 •1246 | **Witness** *1985* •1295 | **Wizard of Oz** *1939* •322 •1132 •1252 | **Women** *1939* •349 •588 •691 •692 | **Working Girl** *1988* •337 •419 | **Working Girls** *1986* •485 | **World Is Not Enough** *1999* •1008 | **Y Tu Mama Tambien** *2001* •477 | **Year of Living Dangerously** *1982* •33 | **You Can't Take It With You** *1938* •350 | **You Only Live Twice** *1967* •1014 | **Young Frankenstein** *1974* •791 | **Young Man of Manhattan** *1930* •1249 | **Zelig** *1983* •671 | ≠